Seven Silent Witnesses

by
Cheryl Lynn Bramlett

Finding Freedom Through
The Power of Forgiveness

15 14 13 12 10 9 8 7 6 5 4 3 2 1

Seven Silent Witnesses
ISBN: 978-1-936521-08-1
Copyright © 2012 by Cheryl Lynn Bramlett

Published by:
Cheryl Lynn Bramlett
P.O. Box 8394
Fayetteville, AR 72704
sevensilentwitnesses@yahoo.com

TABLE OF CONTENTS

Introduction..5

Family Tree 7

Chapter 1..9

Chapter 2..23

Chapter 3..29

Chapter 4..49

Chapter 5..61

Chapter 6..75

Chapter 7..87

Chapter 8..95

Chapter 9..115

Chapter 10..133

Chapter 11..151

Chapter 12..169

Chapter 13..193

Chapter 14..211

Chapter 15..231

Chapter 16..251

Chapter 17..255

Chapter 18..273

Chapter 19..281

INTRODUCTION

An unspoken alliance among seven siblings was the powerful lock that kept the horrible atrocities of abuse enclosed in the individual subconscious mind of each child. Though the decision to stay mute was never discussed, the silence was so practiced that even after reaching adulthood they never considered talking about it – even to each other.

Each of the seven children suffered the devastation and destruction of some type of abuse –physical, sexual, mental and verbal, and neglect. Each dealt with their experiences uniquely. All seven grew into adult survivors of abuse. They had witnessed the abuses of their brothers and sisters, yet they remained silent through the years…until the day when one child dared to break the silence. Pain and suffering tolerated and left unvoiced for years flooded forth that day in an overpowering torrent of memories for each of the seven. The book you're holding today is their story.

As the oldest of the seven children, this book is written based on my memories to help the reader see into the heart and soul of the abused and the abusers. Although my siblings and I have conversed about the events that took place in our childhoods, details of events are written to the best of my memory alone. Names have been changed to protect those involved in this account.

The experiences in the following pages haunted me for many

5

years, but I'm grateful that the story does not end there. In spite of a horrific childhood, I found that there could be hope and peace in life. Could that really be possible?

For anyone who has known abuse of any type, I hope you'll see that your past doesn't have to forever negatively affect your future. You no longer have to silently endure your pain. No matter what you've been through, there is healing for you, too. Believe me, I know.

Cheryl Lynn Bramlett

FAMILY TREE

Maternal Grandparents
Nathan and Mary Cutter

Paternal Grandparents
Hank and Anna Morgan

Father
Clarence Edward Morgan (Renny)

Mother
Mary Beatrice Morgan (Bea)

Children:

1. Cheryl   (Cheryl)
2. Davey   (David)
3. Eddie   (Edward)
4. Richie   (Richard)
5. Kati   (Katrina)
6. Kari   (Karoline)
7. Rosie   (Rosalind)

ONE

The Family Background

BEA

December 2, 1952, was a cold, wintry night in northern New Hampshire. Dr. Dwyer had left some medication to ease Mary Cutter's pain. He cautioned Bea and her brother, George, about leaving their mother alone. Bea had heard Dr. Dwyer say that cancer doesn't hurt until it's too late. Her mother had been in pain for many weeks.

George walked over to the fireplace and added wood to the fire. It seemed futile. The cold in the room refused to be driven out by the flickering heat phantoms rising from the flames. Bea sat stiffly on the edge of her mother's deathbed. Though it was getting dark, neither bothered to switch on the light.

Heads bowed with the heaviness of impending death, the brother and sister sat lost in their own thoughts. Bea was angry with her mother for deserting them in death, yet almost anxious for her to die. She condemned herself for her feelings, yet believed they were justified. George felt awkward with the mixture of emotions welling up inside him. Love and hate are a curious mixture when centered on the same person.

Mary Cutter had always been very cruel to both her children, but especially to Bea. Bea's father, Nathan, had abandoned the family sixteen years earlier when Bea was born. Mary blamed Bea. She often told Bea that upon seeing her at birth, Nathan had said, "She's so ugly; she can't be mine." And with that declaration he'd disappeared – forever.

She was a strong, domineering woman who stood almost six feet tall. She seemed to her children to be fearless though she herself struck fear in every child for miles around. Mary was cruel, often beating her children with a razor strop then forcing them to wash the open wounds with salted water. She seemed to delight in terrorizing them with beatings, starvation, with animals and shame, disgrace and humiliation in front of family and friends.

Mary expressed no fear of death. She was a self-proclaimed atheist and believed the death of humans to be no different than the death of any animal. Bea could only remember one instance of her mother showing alarm or fear. Mary had opened the back door one evening to feed the old yellow farm dog and instead was confronted with a skunk. She screamed, slammed the door shut, and ran through the house shrieking. Bea and George had gleaned a few precious pleasurable moments of private laughter upon every remembrance of that one moment of exposed weakness in Mary Cutter.

Looking upon the gray, pathetic, wretched shell of their mother on her deathbed it seemed doubtful that this could be the same woman who had been their tormentor for so many years.

The lazy flickering of the flames, the stillness of the room, and the hushed atmosphere eventually lulled Bea and George to sleep. When the morning dampness and creeping light of dawn roused them, they found that mercifully in the night, Mary Cutter had stepped over into eternity.

Immediately after the graveside services, George went to live with Uncle Nels in Baltimore. It was to be the last time the brother and sister would see each other for over twenty years. Bea was shipped off to West Virginia to live with Aunt Francis. Within a few months she was to meet and elope with Clarence (Renny) Morgan, by whom she would bear seven children, four girls and three boys.

RENNY

Clarence Edward Morgan was raised by his parents, Hank and Anna Morgan, in the rolling hills of West Virginia. He had one younger brother, Richard. Hank and Anna had both been raised on farms, each with a dozen brothers and sisters. Hank was a hard-working, honest coal miner, yet a very loving and sensitive man. Anna worked hard on the small farm and raised the two boys while Hank stayed down in the mines.

Anna resented her lot in life. As the oldest of twelve children, she had been burdened with the enormous responsibility of caring for them and her perpetually frail and sickly mother. The youngest of the twelve were twin boys, also very frail and unhealthy. Anna dutifully cared for all the children, but she deeply resented the demands placed upon her. Her responsibilities forced her to withdraw from school in the sixth grade. Marriage didn't provide the escape she'd hoped for from hard work and "women's duties." The bitterness embedded in her heart flourished like the enormous vegetable gardens and flowerbeds she toiled over.

Richard (R.J.) was her favorite son, and Clarence ("Renny" to his friends) recognized it. He soon grew as bitter and resentful as his mother. Somehow he developed serious problems with pornography and indecent exposure. Much to the dismay and financial hardship of his parents, Renny was in trouble with the law over it from the time he reached adolescence. He theorized that he felt so drawn to deviant sexual behavior because his mother seemed to abhor even the mention of sex. So loathsome were his mother's expressions about sex that it was puzzling to him how he and his brother had ever been conceived.

Renny also held a bizarre fascination for pain responses from animals. He would torture little animals almost every day. Though after each incident he would resolve to never again hurt an animal, it seemed he was compelled to repeatedly experiment with new tortures. Inevitably, soon he seldom felt any remorse about his sexual behavior or the cruelty to animals. It seemed the pleasure it furnished him justified the behavior.

He was surprised at himself when he could spawn a fleeting moment of tenderness or compassion toward anyone or any living thing. Renny had a knowing within himself that he needed to nurture those sentiments and gravitated toward those he felt could help him. A trip to a church spring break youth camp granted him his desire. It was there that he met Bea. It was the spring of 1953. Renny was almost 18 and Bea had just celebrated her 19th birthday.

MARRIAGE AND FAMILY

In a whirlwind three-day courtship, Renny and Bea "fell in love." Bea's cousin and her husband, several years older than Bea, volunteered to be witnesses at their elopement. With their help Renny and Bea obtained necessary documents to get legal papers for the wedding ceremony. The cooperative cousin had an ulterior motive. She had been annoyed when Bea had come to live with her mother and dad and seized the opportunity to eliminate Bea from her life and oust her from her parents' household.

Bea's relatives were displeased with the match. They felt she had married beneath her – a simple farm boy. Aunt Francis said there was just something about him she didn't trust. Renny was over six feet tall and wore a size eleven shoe, but he didn't weigh over 150 pounds. He was very fair skinned and sunburned easily. His hair was thinning on the top of his head (from repeatedly being sunburned, his mother said.) The hair he had was pale blond, almost white, and very curly. Renny's most noticeable feature was his eyes. They were the first detail anyone noticed about him. They were pale, virtually translucent blue and had an almost haunting quality. Bea was very attracted to Renny's fair coloring.

At five feet two inches and ninety-eight pounds, Bea appeared very diminutive next to Renny. She was as dark as he was fair. Often she was asked if there was Indian blood in her ancestry because of her raven black hair and enormous dark brown eyes. The irises of her eyes were so dark that the definition of the pupils was obscured. People often remarked that obviously in their case "opposites did attract."

Hank and Anna Morgan were as displeased with their new

13

daughter-in-law as Bea's relatives had been about Renny. Realizing an annulment would be useless since Renny would be of age in a few weeks, the Morgans decided to make the best of an unfortunate situation.

With the Morgans' help, Renny and Bea bought a small house trailer and set it up on his parents' farm. It would have been a close call to determine which woman disliked the other more – Bea or Anna. Bea kept hostility seething against Anna, who kept the fire lit under Bea's anger by constantly criticizing her background, appearance, housekeeping and cooking. Nothing Bea did was good enough for Anna's son. Anna hated this "older woman" Bea, who was so provocative and presumptuous. Bea had dared to take this woman's son so swiftly and without warning. It was an unforgiveable transgression.

Both Bea and Renny were visionaries and imagined themselves soon to be in much more luxurious living conditions. They joked about their champagne taste on a beer budget. Renny took a job selling vacuums door to door, and Bea worked in the local nursing home as an aide. Their dreams of wealth and a leisurely, luxurious lifestyle disintegrated when in less than three years' time Renny and Bea had three children. The firstborn was Cheryl, and then came David ("Davey") and Edward ("Eddie"). Bea found it too exhausting and troublesome to keep up with the demands of three children under three – so she just gave up.

She left them to fend for themselves while she escaped into the void of a make-believe world of romance novels, daydreaming, and long hours of sleep. She had given up her job after Cheryl's birth, declaring that, like Renny's mother, she was going to stay home and raise her children. Bea had never been taught house-keeping or cooking. To outsiders she seemed oblivious to the chaotic condition of her home. Childcare was also so overwhelming and all consuming that Bea gave up trying.

Angry over her own failures, she took out her unhappiness on the children. Bea started physically and verbally abusing them by neglect and uncontrollable outrages. Anna and Hank would periodically come over and clean the mounds of garbage and dirty dishes from the kitchen. Hank often said over the years, "Don't tell me you can't raise babies on sour milk and in wet diapers. I've seen it for myself." He would go to work on all the dirty bottles and Anna would start doctoring the raw baby bottoms and scrubbing the huge stacks of diapers and other laundry.

Hank and Anna were astonished when Renny and Bea announced that Bea was pregnant again. It was another boy. They named him Richard (after Renny's brother) and called him "Richie."

Though they never accepted Bea, the Morgans loved their grandchildren. Bea knew the children were her connection to the family life she so craved, but she barely tolerated the grandparents' intrusion into her home. Besides, she was too weary to protest. She spent her days in the bed or on the sofa seldom motivated enough to even dress or bathe herself after Eddie's birth. She longed for Anna to demonstrate some concern or affection toward her, but it never happened.

On the surface, one would never imagine Bea had a desire for any type of relationship with her mother-in-law. Bea had never been nurtured by a mother's love and she longed for what

15

she'd never experienced. Anna was not discerning nor interested enough in Bea's feelings to take thought of her needs. She merely saw an increasingly lazy woman ignoring her husband and neglecting and abusing her children. After only five years of marriage, when Renny announced Bea was pregnant with a fifth child, Anna decided it was time to take some legal action for her grandchildren's sake.

Anna misjudged her son's loyalty to his wife. After the first visit to the couple from the welfare department, Renny loaded up his pregnant wife, all four little children, and abruptly moved away in the night. It was the last Hank and Anna saw of them for almost three years.

THE ROAD TO THE PENITENTIARY

Renny packed the trunk of the '57 Chevy with all the clothing and diapers he could cram into it. He could feel his heartbeat pulsate in his ears and pound in his head. Little did he know that this night was the start of years of hastily loading children and belongings into the car and driving away into the darkness to yet another new beginning.

Knowing he was cutting himself off from his parents stirred anxiety within Renny. What if he couldn't control his problems with pornography and exposure? Hank wouldn't be there to bail him out and pay off the lawyers and courts. Renny desperately wanted to be in control of his behavior, but attempts at "normality" had always ended in failure. Maybe getting away from his mother would help him get in control. Anna's domineering, controlling conduct seemed to drive him to the behaviors.

The desire to be a stable provider like his dad seemed impossible to achieve, and it was never enough anyway. Bea always wanted more than he had been able to provide. She wanted fancy clothes, a big house, a new car, a maid… the list went on. Renny wanted a Cadillac, big diamonds and power. The only control he had was his authority and power over the children. But, they were so little so they didn't present much of a challenge to him.

Bea was certainly a challenge though! She could be very brutal to him verbally. He had become accustomed to verbal cruelties from his mother but felt more threatened by Bea's harsh criticism. Escape from the law and his parents' custody suit was going to produce a by-product he hadn't thought of until now. A new state, home and job would provide opportunity for him to develop some new relationships. He could establish new contacts for his "get rich quick" schemes and maybe he could find a girlfriend, a different, more stimulating companion. He needed someone who understood all the stress he had to endure. He was on his own now and it was definitely time to grow up. He was tired of his parents dictating his life. He was in command now, the master of his own fate at twenty-three years old.

They settled in South Dakota. A few months after they arrived, Katrina ("Kati"), their fifth child and second daughter was born. Renny developed his sales abilities and soon was bringing home a sufficient income to support the family. Still, neither Renny nor Bea was satisfied. Each felt they had been destined for a far grander lifestyle than they could seem to afford.

They soon ran out of credit at the local stores, and the bills were mounting significantly higher every day. They had moved numerous times around the northwest during the two years since they had moved from West Virginia. Now they were headed south to live in New Mexico.

Moving became a habit, partially because they'd get behind in the rent, partially because the garbage and filth would get so insufferable they'd move to start over with a clean apartment or house. They also moved because "the heat was on" Renny for his illegal activities. Making connections into the world of pornographic literature seemed incredibly effortless, and soon Renny was pulled into the profitable realm of handling the sale of the literature. He felt he could justify it. After all, somebody had to profit from the sale of it – why not him? He had so many hungry mouths to feed and a wife with a ravenous appetite for luxury items. Now, at the age of twenty-four, Renny and Bea had five children. Cheryl was now five years old, Davey was four, Eddie had just turned three, Richie was two, and Kati was just over a year old.

They'd only been in New Mexico a short time when Bea discovered she was pregnant with a sixth child. There was a traveling evangelist that Bea had met in South Dakota that she kept up with. She explained to Renny that she needed some "spiritual support." Renny didn't like Rev. Hyatt, but he tolerated him because at least Bea would get out of bed and get dressed up when he came to town. The "Rev." turned out to be a reliable client for Renny's pornographic literature, too.

Renny was gone "on the road" a lot making his connections. He figured it was good for Bea to have a man around when he was gone – for protection. Now that Bea was pregnant again, he was suspicious of the fine evangelist. According to his calculations it seemed doubtful that this baby could be his. He grilled Bea until she got hostile and hit him. Since he couldn't prove anything, Renny decided it would be best to drop the subject. Bea could make life terribly unpleasant for him if he didn't. He figured time would tell.

The desire to escape all the screaming, demanding children, the filth and misery of the house, and loneliness motivated Renny to expand his "business." If he could get a big house and a maid for Bea, then maybe they could escape the children sometimes and be happy again. He wished he could just sell them, or give them away, but he knew Hank and Anna would never forgive him. He knew Anna would compare him to his brother R.J. and recite the wonderful attributes that R.J. possessed and Renny lacked. R.J. had never been able to produce grandchildren for Hank and Anna though. Renny had given them five, soon to be six. He guessed he'd go ahead and claim the sixth. What was the difference anyway?

His greed and hurry to expand the pornography business and make more money caused him to throw away his usual caution. It proved to be a fatal mistake. In the early morning hours a few weeks later, loud pounding at the front door awakened the household. Renny stumbled out of bed and turned on a light. Immediately the entire house was illuminated with floodlights from the outside. Through the sheer curtains Renny could see the house was surrounded by police.

In shock, he opened the front door and several officers exploded into the room, guns drawn. Renny surrendered and was led away in handcuffs. He felt disgraced and ashamed when he glanced back behind him to see Cheryl standing frightened and wide-eyed in the hallway. She was holding baby Kati. To her right in another doorway stood his pregnant wife, and clinging to her nightgown were the other three children. Everyone was crying. Renny choked back tears himself as he was hustled roughly out the door and into a waiting police car.

A few hours later Bea's neighbor came with a phone message from Renny's parents. Renny had called them and he was being extradited back to South Dakota on robbery and pornography charges. They were wiring money for her and the children to come to South Dakota. Hank and Anna would be forced to sell their farm to pay Renny's legal fees.

By early evening Bea had loaded all five children and a German shepherd into the car. Packed into a small trailer behind the car were all the belongings she could squeeze in. It was a long journey for a twenty-seven-year-old pregnant woman with five young children. She knew there was no way she could ask for help from her relatives. It would be impossible to concede that they had been right about Renny.

Certainly she couldn't trust Renny's parents for too much help. After all, they'd tried to take the children away from her. She didn't need anybody anyway. She wasn't going to risk showing any weakness or dependent nature around Renny's folks. No, she was definitely on her own. She'd have to rely on them to get there and get settled, but that was it. She'd get on government help before she'd allow herself to be controlled and domineered by Renny's mother.

With Bea's refusal to accept their help with housing, Hank

and Anna helped Bea get settled in a duplex owned by the government housing authority. They used some of the money from the sale of the farm to make a down payment on a modest two-story white frame house for themselves in another small town, just a few miles away.

Renny was sentenced to ten years in the penitentiary as penalty for various criminal charges. Parole seemed unlikely for several years. It seemed a very dismal future for the Clarence and Bea Morgan family.

Not long after the trial, Karoline was born. It had been a difficult pregnancy for Bea, and during delivery she was told that the baby would probably be stillborn. Bea was greatly relieved to hear a faint cry in the early morning hours shortly after the baby was delivered. She named the baby Karoline Joy because of a psalm she had read the night before that said, "Weeping may endure for a night, but joy cometh in the morning." Karoline was soon shortened to "Kari," and Bea and Kari went home to a full house of five siblings anxiously awaiting the arrival of their new baby sister.

Bea began to rely more heavily on Cheryl, who was now six and a half. Cheryl took on the responsibilities with pride, feeling very grown up. As she tended to her new little sister, she imagined that she was the mother and Kari was her own little baby. She threw away her rag doll. She didn't need that old thing anymore.

There were things that Cheryl and her brothers and sisters did need. The lack of material provision was not particularly detrimental to any of the children. Lack of the basic essential emotional elements of peace, hope, self-worth, joy, and most of all – love – could have destroyed all of them. Several years later, after

21

Renny got out of prison, a seventh child, a girl they named Rosalind (nick-named Rosie) was born.

Somehow all seven children survived the years of abuse and lack and grew up. After a lifetime of silence, Cheryl resolved to break the family cycle of abuse.

Two

Cheryl

A fleeting image of Helen Keller flashed through Cheryl's mind as she stood on the platform acknowledging the thunderous applause from the audience. Helen Keller was right: you could feel the applause of a large audience through your feet.

She had just finished sharing her triumph over the negative circumstances she and all of her brothers and sisters had been subjected to. Now she could be labeled a "survivor of abuse" and was often called upon to speak for church and civic organizations.

Cheryl was now a grown woman. Thirty years had passed since that night in New Mexico when she stood frightened in the hallway as she watched her father being led away by the police. She was grateful for the course her life had taken after she ran away from home at seventeen. The more she shared her experiences and counseled other victims of abuse, the more disconnected she became from her own past.

At first she felt very embarrassed and humiliated revealing how she had been abused as a child. However, it became easier with each speech. She descended from the podium and stepped to the back to greet the people as they left the auditorium. It was always the same wherever she spoke. People wanted to express to her how inspired and blessed they were to see the end result of how her life had transpired. Most significant to Cheryl were the many people, young and old, that took her hand and related to her (usually with tear- glistened faces) how they too had experienced death in the midst of life through abuse. The most heartwarming words to her were, "If you can forgive, then I can, too."

It seemed she had somehow been divinely entrusted with the means to make a difference in other people's lives. Of the hundreds of women, children and men she listened to, there were six lives she was most interested in. She determined that she would do everything possible to help repair the damage produced in the lives of her three brothers -- Davey, Eddie and Richie -- and three sisters -- Kati, Kari and Rosie.

Cheryl had many conversations with her siblings about their growing up time. Often those did not go well, and caused strife. She had to keep a mindset of the real goal of the talks. "We're not here to fight each other. We're here to fight the past. We're here to fight the results of abuse."

"Abuse produces Anger, Bitterness, Unforgiveness, Suffering and Evil. We cannot turn on each other. Our love for each other was a key to our survival. Now let it be a key to our restoration."

This initial conversations that broke the years of silence didn't go at all the way she'd envisioned it, but nonetheless it was a start. She knew it was going to be a long journey to a desired finish.

It seemed it had only served to stir up bad memories. The

central message she wanted to focus on was forgiveness and getting past the abuse. It was as if they had edited out that part of the conversations. What Cheryl had meant as a big healing process initially was a huge mess. Everyone was stirred up. There was so much strife among the brothers and sisters.

Up until this "moment of truth" and opening up conversations with her siblings, Cheryl had felt quite qualified to help people get free of the cycle of abuse. Whenever she spoke to a crowd, the message always seemed effective for the audiences. If, however, it was going to be a miserable failure with her own family, it seemed hardly what she would call a success.

Cheryl knew forgiveness worked. It had for her. She couldn't explain how though. She wasn't any different from her brothers and sisters. She'd tried drugs (valium and percodan), run away from home, and experienced murderous anger toward her parents. She had been self-destructive and had battled suicidal tendencies in her life. She had been very, very angry and consumed with bitterness.

The emotional poverty of her childhood had been diminished with some exceptional friendships experienced since leaving home. Several people had come into her life and provided Cheryl with some guidance and instruction and a taste of what a loving relationship should be. Even these relationships, though, had not been enough to cover the scars of a lifetime.

Forgiveness had helped to produce mental and emotional health and stability in every area of her life. It was vital for her to be able to communicate effectively to her brothers and sisters so they too could experience freedom from their past. She so wanted to see their wounded hearts healed. It seemed it would take a miracle.

She believed she had been brought through for a special purpose. The primary purpose was to help her brothers and sisters. Obviously, it wasn't going to be that easy. She'd have to convince them that they had much to gain by choosing to "accentuate the positive and eliminate the negative."

It truly would take a miracle, but she believed in miracles. The next few months were spent in long, intimate visits, letters, and telephone conversations among the Morgan brothers and sisters. Though each had fragmented memories, collectively they were able to mostly reconstruct their childhood.

Cheryl started a journal written in third person and began arranging the memories in chronological order. She tried to incorporate pieces of everyone's memories and emotions into the journal. If she could get all the kids to open up and share their wounds, she felt that somehow it would be a healing balm and the conclusion would be "and they all lived happily ever after."

Meanwhile, there was a lot to deal with for each of them. If they could give voice to the sense of powerlessness and feelings of betrayal that the abuse had produced, then perhaps the confusion of fragmented memories would become ordered in their minds and would produce order in their lives.

The ultimate product of abuse and a horrible consequence of their experiences seemed to be an underlying perception of rejection. It seemed all the children had become emotionally desensitized and vulnerable to destructive relationships. Cheryl's greatest desire was to see them transported out of the past to face the truth.

She knew that just simply burying the past allowed it to still poison the soul. It had to be dug out and the empty places cleaned and healed. The journal was going to be a part of the key to that healing.

THREE
THE JOURNAL

Cheryl stood at the screen door looking out onto the front porch. At five years old, she was just tall enough to reach the door handle. Her family had finally settled into a home somewhere up north since the short time they had left West Virginia.

It was dusk, and June bugs were colliding into the screen, against the light, and buzzing upside down on the porch floor of their home. Somewhere in the background babies were crying, but Cheryl didn't worry about it. The little girl across the street had told Cheryl that she knew how to make chocolate shakes. Cheryl had never tasted one and was anxious to try it. The little girl had said, "When my mommy goes out to sit in the porch swing with my daddy, you can come over and we'll make the shakes."

Cheryl's mouth watered in anticipation. Suddenly her friend's mommy's silhouette appeared in the doorway across the street. Cheryl waited until she'd settled comfortably in the swing, then she raced out the door. The houses were very close together with lawns that went straight up from the street to the front porches. They were so steep that the walkways to the front door were steps all the way up.

Cheryl opted to skip all those steps by dropping to the ground and rolling all the way down the hill. Picking herself up, she ran across the street and climbed up the hill to her friend's house. The mommy nodded to her as she slipped in through the screen door, opening it just the tiniest bit to keep the June bugs out.

Her little friend was waiting inside the doorway and beckoned Cheryl to follow her on tiptoe to the kitchen. She grabbed a stool and climbed up to the freezer to get the ice cream to hand down to Cheryl. Next she lifted the heavy glass bottle of milk from the icebox. Cheryl watched the milk foam as her friend poured it into a tall silver tumbler. It looked so white and cold and good.

At Cheryl's home they always had non-fat dry milk. It came in a box, and every morning for breakfast Cheryl would fill a coffee cup with water and stir in a tablespoon of the milk powder. Each child was then allowed one coffee cup of puffed wheat cereal that came in a big bag. In the winter months the puffed wheat was replaced with hot oatmeal, which was somewhat more palatable. Cheryl would carefully pour milk on the cereal, saving some to drink.

She didn't like the taste of it but learned she got hungry if she didn't drink it. All the kids detested the smell of puffed wheat (except Davey), but they knew they'd better eat it because there was nothing else until lunch. Mama and Daddy always had two fried eggs, bacon or sausage, toast and coffee for breakfast. The children were never allowed to taste it, and any scraps were fed to the dogs.

Lunch was always commodity peanut butter and grape jelly sandwiches on thin white sandwich bread. It was Cheryl's job to make the sandwiches. She inevitably tore the bread on at least one sandwich. That would automatically be her sandwich. Davey liked his with the peanut butter layer on the bottom, and Richie wanted his jelly layer on the bottom. Cheryl wondered when they'd get smart enough to figure out she just had to turn the sandwich over to change the layers around.

Eddie was very picky. He wanted margarine first, then peanut butter, and then jelly. Next he wanted the crust cut off and the sandwich cut in four triangles. Sometimes, to be mean, Cheryl would pretend to forget and she'd cut it in squares. Eddie would pout and not eat for a while, but eventually hunger would win over his principles and he'd eat it anyway. Lunch also included Kool-Aid and sometimes canned tomato or chicken noodle soup. It depended on what the commodities included and what time of the month it was.

Supper was varied with a cycle of goulash, macaroni and cheese, spaghetti, beans and cornbread, or potted meat sandwiches. Saturday nights were a real treat. Mama and Daddy would go out to eat and the kids would get to eat hot dogs and pork and beans. Perhaps the children would never have had a sense of lack had Mama and Daddy eaten the same meals they provided for the children.

Cheryl fixed the hot dogs and beans for the kids while Mama and Daddy went out to eat steak and baked potatoes. The kids ate the hot dogs and pork and beans cold. They didn't know anybody ever cooked them. Davey always ate the white chunks of pork.

Nobody else wanted them.

Sunday dinner was the noon meal. It was always the best of the week. Usually it was commodity Spam with pineapple chunks and brown sugar. They would have mashed potatoes and canned green beans or corn. Cheryl always thought the plates looked so pretty on Sunday with all the colors of food. Mama and Daddy always had pork chops, baked potatoes, and asparagus. Mama said asparagus was too expensive to feed to children. Sometimes on Sundays they had dessert. Chocolate sandwich cookies, applesauce, or Bisquick coffee cake was always a welcome treat.

Cheryl watched now as her friend scooped chocolate ice cream from the box and dropped spoonfuls into the cold, fresh milk. Next she took some powder from a brown jar and added just a little spoonful. She pushed the big silver tumbler onto a machine by the sink and pressed a button on the front of it. Cheryl covered her ears and ran toward the door.

"Don't be scared," her friend called. "It makes that noise every time it gets turned on." Cheryl hesitantly approached the machine again. The silver tumbler was getting frosty on the sides and the frothy white milk was turning smooth and chocolate. Thankfully the noisy machine was finally turned off. The little girl climbed up on the cabinet and stood to reach inside.

She pulled out two colorful aluminum tumblers and tossed them down to Cheryl. Jumping down, she took the big, frosty silver tumbler and poured the thick chocolate shake into one of the small tumblers. As she was pouring the second one, her mommy called to her, "What are you doing in there? Are you making a mess?"

The little girl, startled, jerked around toward her mother's voice. When she did, she knocked over one of the tumblers and the thick chocolate spilled all over the counter and began dripping onto the floor.

Cheryl was terrified. "Your mommy is going to beat us! Hurry, let's hide!" The little girl seemed unconcerned. "Well, the one that spilled was yours," she said. "Come on, help me get a towel and clean this up." Cheryl didn't mind that she didn't get to taste the shake. She just wanted to clean up the mess and get away from the house before the mommy came in and started beating them. "I guess you'd better go home," Cheryl's friend said.

Cheryl bolted back home and slipped into her bed and burrowed under the cover to the bottom of the bed. Curling up into a ball to make herself as tiny as possible, she waited for the inevitable. Surely that mommy was going to tell her mama. She'd come in screaming and waving a belt over her head and start hitting. Cheryl knew that once she got started, Mama wouldn't stop hitting until she got tired of hitting. That always took a long, long time. Cheryl would count as high as she could, then just pray for her to stop or for "The Black" to rescue her.

"The Black" might sound frightening to most little children, but to Cheryl it was a welcome escape. "The Black" would come in waves at first, like the ebb and flow of a tide. It seemed "The Black" got stronger and stronger until finally it would sweep over Cheryl and she could escape the screaming, the hitting, and the pain.

When "The Black" would lift it was like waking up from a deep sleep after a violent storm. The air would be calm and silent, but the pain was always still there. Cheryl wished she could make

"The Black" take away the pain, too. She didn't know where "The Black" had come from, but she counted him a necessary friend.

Cheryl never ventured across the street to her friend's house again. She didn't want to chance reminding her friend's mommy of her presence. Luckily, she had escaped a beating. Cheryl felt sorry for her friend. She should have stayed and taken some of the beating for her. But, maybe her friend's mommy hadn't beaten her. That was impossible though. A kid always got a beating for a mistake, even if it was an accident. Cheryl sensed a kinship with her little friend and pledged her undying loyalty to her for suffering a beating in her behalf.

Her friend wasn't allowed to cross the street, so their friendship was confined to waving at each other from the open screen doors. Cheryl knew she would start kindergarten soon. Maybe she could tell her friend how much she valued her sacrifice when they met on the playground. But that conversation was not to be. One night, right before school was to start, Cheryl's daddy, Renny, loaded up Cheryl's mama, Cheryl, Davey, Eddie, Richie and Kati in the car. "Daddy, where are we going?"

"Cheryl, you hush. You'll wake the other kids. We're moving to a new and wonderful life somewhere far away," Renny whispered.

Cheryl settled back in the seat. She liked traveling in the car. Sometimes, even though she fought it, she would fall asleep riding. She would dream that they would just keep on driving forever and ever, never getting home. Coming back home was the only bad part of riding in the car.

The little boys were stirring, trying to get comfortable. Daddy threw a quilt into the back seat and Cheryl adjusted it to cover herself and the three boys. Mama had Kati in the front seat with her, lying between her and Daddy. Mama said she was going to have another baby, but it sure didn't look like it to Cheryl. Her stomach was so flat she just didn't know how a baby could fit in there.

A lady once told Cheryl that babies are found in a cabbage patch. Cheryl didn't believe it though. She'd seen Mama's tummy get really big, then Mama would go to the hospital and come home with another baby. Her stomach would go back to being flat for a little while until she started growing another baby. Mama didn't like Cheryl asking a lot of questions, so Cheryl kept quiet and watched. She was proud of herself that on her own she'd figured out how the doctor got the baby out.

She had watched Mama and noticed that the bigger her tummy got, Mama's bellybutton would change. When Mama got really big, her bellybutton would stick out. Sometimes it could be seen sticking out even under her maternity smock. Cheryl figured the bellybutton would finally explode open and then Daddy would rush Mama to the hospital. The doctor would reach in and lift the baby out. Then he would take special instruments and tuck Mama's bellybutton back the way it was before and she'd be ready to come home.

Mama and Daddy often told Cheryl she was ugly, but they usually agreed she was pretty smart. Even when they'd make her stand in the corner and say "I am stupid" a hundred times, she still knew inside that she was actually pretty smart.

Cheryl had drifted off to sleep, but as she was jolted awake, she suddenly realized that the car had stopped. Rising up, she saw Daddy hanging up a gas pump. Renny caught her eye as he turned around.

"Bea!" he tapped on his wife's window. "Get that kid down!" Daddy was hollering, but in a whisper. Bea swung her arm wildly in a blind sweep of the backseat. Cheryl dodged her hand.

"Cheryl, stay down! It's the middle of the night," Bea whispered. Her voice sounded strange. Not because it was a loud whisper. There was something odd about it. Cheryl raised her head just enough so that her eyes were at the bottom of the backseat window. She could see her daddy twisting the knob on the gas station door. Everything was very dark. Couldn't he see the station was closed?

"Mama," Cheryl ventured to say, "How could Daddy get gas? The station is closed."

"Cheryl, this is the last time I'm going to tell you. Lay down! Now!"

"But, Mama..."

"Cheryl, he's leaving a note for the man and leaving him money. Now lay down, or else!" Bea warned.

Cheryl knew better than to pursue anything once Bea said "or else." She slid back down in the seat. Hiding her face in the quilt, she pretended to be asleep as Renny slid back into the car.

"Did you get anything?" Bea leaned close to whisper in Renny's ear.

"Not enough. There's a Dairy Queen down the block. I think I'll try there." In a few minutes he eased the car to a stop and noiselessly slipped out the door. Cheryl carefully and slowly raised up and peered out into the darkness.

She could see Renny in a crouched position moving stealthily across the parking lot along a line of hedges. He worked at pulling on some kind of board or piece of metal on the side of the building near the ground.

Cheryl's heart was pounding. She didn't know why she was scared, but the air was thick with fear. At last Daddy pulled the piece off the building and, lying on his back, slid head first inside. Cheryl watched his feet disappear into the building. Straining her eyes into the darkness, she watched anxiously for him to reappear. Bea's breathing in the front seat was quick and shallow. Cheryl concentrated on breathing only once for every two times Mama breathed. At last Daddy reappeared, and in the same crouched position he dashed back to the car, carrying a wadded up paper sack. "Give me that sack," Bea demanded. "Drive away deliberate and slow, then let's hit the highway." Cheryl could hear the sack rattle with change. She knew it was a sack of money.

* * *

Just a few weeks before, Cheryl had been in the drugstore with her mother. There was a big square display box built around the cash register right by the door. Precisely at Cheryl's eye level were bins of penny candy. Mama was talking with the man and paying for her nerve medicine. All Cheryl could see was a gigantic bin of Tootsie rolls. The sign above it said "2 for 1 cent." Before she knew what she was doing, she reached in the box and took two Tootsie rolls. They were so long they stuck out the ends of her clenched fist. There was no turning back now. She had to run. Cheryl ran out of the store and stood on the sidewalk three doors down waiting nervously for her mama.

Cheryl wished she had a penny to take to the man at the cash register. In Sunday school they taught that it was wrong to steal. It was one of God's ten most important rules. They sang a song in church that said, "When the role is called up yonder I'll be there." The Sunday school teacher said that if you broke one of God's ten rules or commandments, your name wouldn't be called. If your name wasn't called, then you'd have to go to hell.

Hell was a bad, bad place. The teacher said it was worse than anything ever on earth. It was hot and there was fire and hot coals and you'd burn forever. Cheryl thought of all the worst things on earth and she knew without a doubt she sure didn't want to go to hell.

One time Mama had gotten mad and she had held Cheryl over the kitchen stove. It was a big black stove that always had a blue teakettle on top. On one side there was a handle that stuck up. Cheryl was getting strong enough that she could lift the handle. It was hooked onto a big, round, black circle. When that was lifted off Mama would have Cheryl throw corncobs into the hole, or sometimes coal. Once when Mama got mad she held Cheryl over the hole and told her she was going to drop her down into the fire if she was ever naughty again.

Mama had made a believer out of Cheryl many times and left no doubt in her mind that she could -- and would -- drop her into the fire if she got mad enough. If hell was worse than that, Cheryl knew she couldn't stand it. The more she thought about it, the more fear consumed her. The fear of hell was greater than the terror of confessing to Mama.

Mama walked out of the store and Cheryl ran up to her. "Mama, Mama, I took these Tootsie rolls. I'm sorry. Please don't let me go to hell." Mama jerked Cheryl up by one arm, and dangling her, stomped back into the store and sat Cheryl down hard on the counter in front of the man at the cash register.

"I'm ashamed to say we have a little thief here," Mama told the man. Cheryl was mortified that Mama was talking so loudly. "You can take her and do with her whatever you want," Mama said to the man.

Cheryl's heart hammered in her chest. Mama had told other men to take her and they touched her in ways she didn't like, then they gave Mama money. She squeezed her eyes shut and waited for what the man would do. Feeling his big hands encircle her waist, she prayed for "The Black" to come and swallow her up. To her astonishment he sat her on his lap and patted her hand that was still clutching the Tootsie rolls. They had flattened out now under the warmth and pressure of her fist.

"What's your name, sweetheart?"

"Cheryl."

"Cheryl, do you have a penny?"

"No, sir."

"Can you read yet?"

"A little, sir. I help my Mama at the grocery store and with coupons. We sometimes get pennies for coupons I find."

"Did you see the sign that said those Tootsie rolls are two for one penny?"

"Yes, sir."

"Cheryl, if you knew they were two for one penny and you

didn't have a penny, why did you take the Tootsie rolls?"

"I don't know."

"Well, this is very serious. If you steal something when you're bigger, the police will come and take you to prison. Now, I don't think a nice little girl like you would like to be in prison, would you?"

"No, sir." Cheryl was terrified. Mama and Daddy said if the police came they would take you and lock you away in a dungeon, a big deep hole. They'd lock you away down there and you would never get to see your Mama or Daddy or brothers or sisters ever again. All you'd ever get to eat was bread and water. Her heart was pounding so rapidly now that she knew "The Black" was coming to help her escape.

Far away she heard the man say, "Cheryl. Cheryl? If you can tell me you're really sorry, I'll forgive you and let you go. But you must promise me you'll never steal anything ever again. Can you promise me that?"

"The Black" withdrew as Cheryl grasped what the man was saying. She found her voice and emphatically promised she would never, ever steal anything again. The man lifted her back over the counter and set her feet down on the floor. As she looked back up at him, she thought, He must be an angel.

Her angel looked down at her and said, "Don't ever forget this day, Cheryl. Remember, too, that if you're sorry for what you do, Jesus will forgive you just like I did."

"I will, sir. Yes, sir." With great relief and restored dignity, Cheryl walked out of the store with her mama. She turned and looked back at the man, straight into his eyes. Hoping her eyes conveyed the message, she said in her heart, "I love you, thank you, and I'll never forget you."

                                               * * *

Mama's voice interrupted Cheryl's memory. "Well, Renny, I think we've got enough to hold us for a little while."

"Do you think we can settle inconspicuously in some little town further south or west?" Renny asked Bea.

"I think so. We should be somewhere safe sometime tomorrow night. Let's pull over and sleep for awhile."

Cheryl measured her breathing so they wouldn't detect she was awake. Daddy had stolen some money – a lot of money. Now they were going to live in another place. Cheryl didn't know where they were headed, but from Sunday school she knew that "south" was at the bottom of the world. If Daddy and Mama weren't careful they'd all fall off the bottom of the world into hell. She sure hoped they planned to return that money soon so they could get forgiven before they ended up in prison or hell.

Renny finally pulled off the main highway and drove a short distance down a side road before pulling over. By now Cheryl had been sleeping almost an hour. The baby and the little boys also were sound asleep. Bea stirred as Renny shut down the motor. "I'm cold, Renny. Can you get a blanket out of the trunk?"

"Sure." Renny felt a chill as he stepped out into the night air. He didn't know if it was the night air or a slight sense of fear. This was the first time he had stolen anything. The decision to leave had been so sudden that he hadn't been prepared. He hadn't had time to sell any of his pornographic literature and it would take a little time to tap into a new market in another state.

He had a wife and five hungry mouths to feed. Selling vacuum cleaners door to door was a wretched way to make a living for that many people. Now Bea was pregnant again. Renny was annoyed with her for not being more cautious. In fact, he couldn't figure out how in the world it had happened. He had been traveling during the week most of the time.

There was a traveling evangelist Bea kept up with that sometimes spent the night. One night when Renny was really tired he dared question Bea about Rev. Hyatt insinuating maybe there was a little more to the relationship than just friendship. Bea became very hostile and even slapped Renny. He decided to let it drop. It probably was his anyway. Sometimes he wondered if she felt she needed to stay pregnant or he'd force her to work. Who could afford that many children anyway?

Bea didn't know it, but Renny had tried to sign up for military service. Every branch of the military had turned him down because he had responsibility for so many little brats. The man at the recruiting office said they'd have to pay him like a major with that many dependents. No way would the government take on a burden like that. It was oppressive to have the burden of so many; Bea didn't have any compassion on him for the load he was carrying. She felt she was carrying a heavy load herself.

Renny knew they both expressed their anger with their own unhappiness by being unreasonably harsh with the children. He wished they didn't have to be so strict, but Bea had shown him that with five children it was absolutely necessary to rule with an iron hand. He wished he could have gotten into the service before they'd had so many children. Maybe then he could have learned how to better handle so many children – and how to handle Bea. Renny closed the trunk and climbed back behind the wheel. Bea had already gone back to sleep. She did look rather pretty as the peace of sleep was upon her countenance. He spread the blanket across the front seat and closed his eyes.

* * *

Brilliant sunlight streamed through the car windows illuminating the sleeping faces of the Morgan family. Bea, sensing familiar pressure on her bladder, was the first to stir. Like a slow-motion domino effect, the whole family began to rouse and stretch to ease the stiffness imposed by their cramped sleeping quarters.

Everyone took their turn behind a nearby tree then lined up as Bea handed out cookies and tea for breakfast. Renny was romping in the field with the family dog, a German shepherd named Brutus. Brutus had provided a warm footrest through the night hours for the four sets of little bare feet in the back seat of the car. "Renny, let's go," Bea shaded her eyes with her free hand as she looked into the sun toward her husband. "Come on. All the kids are fed and watered. Let's go."

"Okay, okay. I just had to work out the kinks from being behind the wheel so long." Renny came up beside her, out of breath. "Get in the car, Brutus. Come on kids, pile in."

"Hey! Where's the cat?" Bea anxiously rooted through the backseat. "Where's the cat, kids?"

Davey spoke up. He was four, and like the rest of the children, very small for his age, frail, and fragile looking. His fine hair, almost white, was cut short into a crew cut like his two little brothers' hair. Davey was wearing a white cotton shirt, buttoned wrong,

43

half in and half out of his light green trousers. The trousers rode low with the added weight of six extra inches at the end of each leg that flowed into a heap around each of his ankles. Looking way up at his mama, his head, as usual, tipped toward his right shoulder, and squinting one eye, he boldly said, "Kitty sc'atch me, an' I fro da kitty out da winnow."

Bea swiveled her head around toward Renny, then back to Davey. All the children stood frozen, waiting for her reaction, their eyes wide and unblinking with apprehension and fear of what she would do next. There was a prolonged silence as they waited for her to react.

She drew herself up to her full height, shifting the weight of Kati on her hip. Then, in a loud, exaggerated mimic of Davey, she dramatically repeated his answer, "Kitty sc'atch me an' I fro' da kitty out da winnow." She repeated it again, louder this time. "Kitty sc'atch me an' I fro' da kitty out da winnow!"

Davey slowly backed up a half step at a time toward his older sister, Cheryl. Instinctively he put his hand to his throat knowing he would likely be snapped up by the neck any second now. He couldn't hear anything anymore.

Bea was moving closer to him, her mouth opening wide and closing again as she mockingly repeated his phrase. He shrunk back further and further. Suddenly he fell over backward onto the ground. He knew now he'd probably be stomped and kicked. He instinctively drew his knees in to his chest. Renny reached down with one gigantic hand and scooped him up off the ground. To Davey's amazement, Renny started laughing.

The children looked back and forth one to another not knowing how to react. Renny and Bea started chanting back and forth, "Kitty sc'atch me an' I fro' da kitty out da winnow!"

Bea was laughing so hard now she had to set baby Kati down on the hood of the car.

All the children were laughing. It was a wonderful feeling to laugh. They were hugging each other and jumping up and down beside the car. Pretty soon everyone was singing a splendid, spontaneous original singsong. "Kitty sc'atch me an' I fro' da kitty out da winnow."

Davey felt a flush of pride in himself. He didn't know exactly what he'd done, but everybody sure was having fun. Bea and Renny finally regained control and repacked the car with children and belongings. Exhausted from their hysterical laughter, everyone was quiet for a while. Bea shook her head, smiling, as she fed Kati a bottle. She chuckled, privately enjoying the humor of it one more time. Renny caught her eye and winked. He looks handsome, Bea thought as she watched the sunlight shining through Renny's thinning blonde curls.

In the back seat Cheryl and the little boys played finger games, passed a little metal car back and forth, and in hushed tones sang fragments of Sunday school songs. Soon the peaceful atmosphere lulled them all to sleep again and Renny and Bea were free to talk.

* * *

They settled in a little town in New Mexico and Renny got a legitimate sales job. On the side he soon had networked a profitable circle of customers interested in paying high prices to satisfy their appetite for pornographic material.

Renny was delighted with himself for being capable and self-sufficient in the support of his growing family. His delight was partially obscured by Bea's taste for "the finer things in life." The inner drive she had for expensive jewelry and clothes and an elegant nightlife quickly consumed the money Renny brought in.

They saved a little by letting Cheryl babysit the children on Friday and Saturday nights when they went out. Renny felt a slight twinge of guilt at giving Cheryl so much responsibility at five years old. There was a gnawing uneasiness in the back of his mind about leaving the children alone for so long. Bea convinced him that children rise up to whatever is required of them. "Cheryl's smart," Bea proclaimed. "She can handle them. They all fall asleep soon after we're gone anyway. It's almost the same as our being there asleep. We don't do anything for them when we're asleep and they are all asleep, now do we?"

Reluctantly Renny agreed and the couple continued their weekend outings. "After all," Bea said, "we deserve some time away from those kids. They'll drive us crazy if we don't, and that would be bad for them." She tossed her long, dark hair back over her shoulder and laughed. Renny laughed too. All those kids did really get on his nerves. His mother had always told him he was a nervous person. Nervous people shouldn't be around that many kids all the time.

Bea was a nervous person, too. That's why she had to take "nerve pills." She went to several doctors in the surrounding towns to get prescriptions from each one. She needed a supply to hold her through the pregnancy. Once she started showing, there was no way they would give her the pills. It was for the good of the kids that Renny and Bea got away. Lord only knows how hard Bea was on them when Renny was away. He'd seen her go almost berserk with whipping them even with him there.

Renny knew he wasn't a perfect parent either. Sometimes he could feel himself go out of control in hitting the children. If they really made him angry he would stomp on them and kick them, or throw them across the room.

He snickered to himself, "Those kids...they are tough. They always get back up and ask for more." Bea always said, "If you don't draw blood, the kid hasn't learned a lesson." Sometimes it took awhile for the belt to draw blood. It worked better using the buckle end of the belt or two belts held together.

He knew Bea was sorry sometimes too, especially on Saturday nights when the children took their baths. Most always they had welts and bruises on their legs, backs and bottoms. Some of the older bruises were greenish yellow, while newer marks were swollen dark purple welts and angry red knots.

Depending on what they'd been hit with there would be hard knots or long streaks with thin scabbed lines outlining the buckle marks. The children would laugh and splash though, and that eased Renny's conscience. After all, Renny and Bea were doing the best they could. That was the most anyone could ask of them. The kids loved them. They were fairly obedient. That's what counted.

FOUR

By the time Cheryl started kindergarten, the Morgan family was settled in their new surroundings in New Mexico. One Saturday during the hot summer, the family next door convinced Bea to entrust Cheryl to them for the afternoon as company for their five-year-old daughter. They had surprised her by taking her to the zoo. Cheryl was delighted with all the sights, sounds, and smells of the zoo. She'd never before experienced the sensation of being filled with the joy and wonder of simply being a carefree child. It had been a wonderful day for Cheryl.

The neighbors had bought an incredible pink treat for her called "cotton candy." It was an amazing delicacy. Cheryl savored it in tiny little bites that evaporated miraculously into a sweet nothingness in her mouth. She stuffed bits of it into her pockets to share later with her brothers and sister. They also bought her a magic balloon. It floated high in the air next to her, attached to her wrist by a long, thin piece of string. Cheryl chose a blue balloon. It was her favorite color. As she skipped along she imagined herself floating high above the world like the beautiful blue balloon.

Too soon it was time to return home. Cheryl was torn. She wanted to stay in this wonderful place with these happy, kind people. She needed to get home to her brothers and sister, though. She wanted to share the wonderful afternoon with them. They would be amazed at the magic balloon floating above her head. She could picture them crowding around her, each waiting patiently for their taste of the wonderful "cotton candy." She was so happy to have something to share with them.

Cheryl worried about the other children when she wasn't home. They looked to her as their leader, their comforter, and their protector. Rarely was she able to protect them from Mama and Daddy when they were angry, but she was able to comfort them and keep them out of a little bit of trouble on occasion. Cheryl knew that the longer she rode in the car, the closer they were to home. It seemed to her that the bright blue sky began to grow overcast.

As they turned down the street toward the house, Cheryl's siblings spotted them instantly. Ignoring warnings and their own past experiences with sand burrs, they ran barefoot off the porch and across the sandy yard to the neighbor's driveway. They were all four waving and smiling and running, excited their sister was back. There was no jealousy, only joy that she got to go. To them it was as if they'd gone themselves if Cheryl went. The Morgan children had developed a tight alliance and fervently loved and protected each other.

Cheryl fought the balloon and the horde of admiring children as she maneuvered out of the car. She grabbed up baby Kati and ran toward the porch. With three little boys pressing around her she almost forgot to thank her benefactors. Suddenly remembering them, she turned and shouted her gratitude across the yard. She sat down on the steps and lowered the balloon so that each child could touch it and peer inside – trying to discover the magic inside that let it float. She showed them again and again how it would rise back up on its own when she loosened the string.

Abruptly she remembered the wonderful "cotton candy" in her pockets. Reaching in, she retrieved the squashed remains of the fluffy little balls she'd preserved. Davey, Eddie, Richie and baby Kati were delighted with the morsels and scavenged her pockets for any missed crumbs. Cheryl enjoyed sharing her experiences with them and their elation more than she had enjoyed the outing – and that was saying a lot!

Then, without warning, somehow the balloon string around her wrist loosened. In an instant her precious magic blue balloon escaped and floated up toward the blue sky and fluffy white clouds. Cheryl was ready to cry when she noticed the boys running excitedly across the yard, following the balloon's ascent. She ran along with them and strained her eyes until it was lost to her. In a way she was happy. She had given the balloon its freedom, though unwillingly.

Someday she was going to find out the magic ingredient that made the balloon float and she and the kids would drink it. What a wondrous thing to be able to float freely away from everything and up into the heavens to God. She wouldn't dream of leaving without Davey and Eddie and Richie and Kati, but they would surely leave Mama and Daddy.

Maybe they wouldn't leave and to be gone forever, but long enough for their parents to miss everybody and be sorry for hurting all the kids. Cheryl knew that all mamas and daddies that love their kids have to hurt them. If they really love their kids, they make them bleed so that they won't be mean and evil kids with the devil in them. Cheryl knew Mama and Daddy had to hurt them, but that didn't make her like that fact.

Later, lying in the bed with the other kids, Cheryl replayed the day's events, reliving the excitement. All the other children were already asleep. Kati was pushed up against her back. I hope those rubber pants don't leak. I hate to wake up wet, Cheryl thought. Cheryl still felt happy inside. She hummed quietly to herself, but that didn't seem to adequately express the joy springing up within. She wished she knew how to whistle. She felt she needed to whistle. Cheryl hadn't heard whistling very often lately. Grandpa Morgan whistled a lot. She missed him. Cheryl concentrated on how Grandpa Morgan looked when he whistled. She worked her mouth around until it felt right, then puffed out her cheeks and blew with all her strength. Nothing came out but a fine mist of spit.

Wiping her mouth, she tried again and again. Her cheeks were beginning to hurt. Suddenly Cheryl got a revelation. "I'll bet you draw your breath in, not out." She tried it, and much to her amazement, it did create a short whistling sound. She practiced again and again then tried blowing the air out. It worked! It worked! It worked! Cheryl began whistling a wildly joyous, instinctive, spontaneously created song. She was so enraptured in her celebration of the day's events and her victory over the whistling challenge that she forgot to be quiet. She didn't hear Renny and Bea come into the room.

Bea shrieked as she flicked on the light, "Stop that ridiculous, insane, tuneless whistling... N-O-W! It's driving me nuts!" Cheryl jerked upright in the bed.

"Renny!" Bea was screaming. "Make that little brat quit glaring at me!" Bea spun around and stomped out of the room. Renny snatched Cheryl up from the bed, raised her above his head, and threw her back onto the bed at full force. Cheryl bounced high and hit the wall. As she dropped back toward the bed, her head jerked backward and her chin caught on the iron railing of the headboard before she fell back onto the bed. She landed on top of the sleeping children who awakened and started crying.

"Shut up and lay back down and go back to sleep, all of you!" Renny demanded. As he reached to switch the light out, he noticed a dark spot on the mattress beside Cheryl's head. Fear clutched him for a moment and he ventured over to the bed for closer inspection. Blood was flowing out one side of Cheryl's mouth.

"Bea... Bea! Get back in here!" Something in Renny's voice made Bea come rushing back in. "Look, what's wrong with her?" Bea pushed him aside. "Oh here, let me take a look. It doesn't look that bad to me." She shook Cheryl. "Cheryl, open your eyes. Open your mouth for Mama."

Cheryl's eyes opened. They looked glazed and were still rolling back into her head. Bea shook her again. "Cheryl, listen to Mama. Open your mouth." Cheryl came to and began screaming. The pain in her mouth was consuming. Her tongue felt gigantic, like it was going to choke her. "Oh, my God! Renny!" Bea exclaimed. "A chunk of her tongue is hanging! What are we going to do?"

"Well, we can't take her to a doctor. Look, her chin is bleeding too. *#!@*, she's got a good egg on her forehead. I'll go get some ice and a washrag. Make her quit screaming!" Renny was hollering above the din. "Make them all shut up!"

With a screamed, strong warning, the younger children quickly lay still in the bed, daring not to move. Renny turned off the bedroom light and left the hall light on to enable them to treat Cheryl's injuries. He and Bea doctored and cleaned up Cheryl's face the best they could. Bea gave her a washrag wrapped around crushed ice.

"Suck on this, Cheryl. It will help the swelling in your tongue go down." Cheryl took the washrag and lay back on the bed with it in her mouth. She reached over and pulled Kati next to her. The little boys had already fallen back to sleep, too. As Bea reached for the door she reprimanded Cheryl, "If you wouldn't act up, these things wouldn't happen to you. You realize that, don't you, Cheryl?"

"Yes, Mama." Cheryl closed her eyes and prayed for sleep to carry away the pain in her mouth and head. She heard Mama and Daddy arguing in the distance. It was a typical backdrop in the night hours. In that familiar atmosphere Cheryl found some comfort and fell asleep with the washrag in her mouth.

* * *

The pain in her tongue awakened Cheryl before the rest of the household. She slipped out of bed and climbed up on the bathroom sink to examine the damage. Blood had dried and congealed all around her mouth. Cheryl didn't have to stick her tongue out to examine it. It was so swollen it hung over her bottom lip. The ugly knot in the center of her forehead was shiny and taking on color. She'd have to be careful so that her bangs would cover that at school. Mama and Daddy would have to come up with an explanation for outsiders of how her tongue had been cut.

Sensing a need to do something to redeem herself, Cheryl went to the kitchen. Fixing breakfast for Mama and Daddy would probably be the best idea. She mixed up the coffee cups of powdered milk for the other children and carefully measured out their daily puffed wheat allocation. Mama and Daddy would have bacon, eggs, and toast. Mama had carefully trained Cheryl on how to fix their bacon and eggs.

The bacon must be fried slowly in the heavy black skillet, and then drained on newspaper. Eggs must be fixed in a separate pan on a low fire with butter. When the eggs were almost done on one side, a little water was poured into the pan and a lid set on top. It had to be checked often. Mama didn't like any runny whites, and Daddy would throw the eggs if the yellows got hard. Timing was everything.

Cheryl's stomach knotted as she finished the bacon and started the eggs. She prayed she would time the eggs just right and be able to get them out of the pan without breaking the yolk. That made Daddy just as angry as a hard yolk.

Smelling breakfast cooking roused everyone and they all came and took their places at the table. Mama and Daddy sat down to their bacon and eggs and toast. The children poured their powdered milk over the puffed wheat. None of them considered asking for bacon and eggs. Mama and Daddy almost always ate a different menu than the children. Cheryl watched everyone eat, waiting for a comment from her parents.

Mama must have perceived Cheryl's apprehension. "Cheryl, sit down and eat, for God sakes. You bother me standing there and staring. And stop trying to look so pitiful with those big, sad bug eyes of yours and your mouth so stupidly hung open." Cheryl lowered her eyes and moved deliberately toward the table. Surely Mama or Daddy would notice how big the knot on her head was, or how swollen her tongue looked.

As if she'd read Cheryl's mind, not bothering to even look up, Mama said, "Don't you expect me to feel sorry for you, little girl. It's your own fault you hurt yourself. You're going to tell anyone that asks that you were jumping up and down on the bed, turned a somersault, and hit your mouth on the iron headboard."

"Okay, Mama." Cheryl tried to take a bite of cereal but felt she was going to choke. There just wasn't room in her mouth for food and a swollen tongue. She sipped on the watery milk.

"I tell you what, kids," Mama suddenly announced. "It's Sunday, and I'm going to let Cheryl make you all some cinnamon toast. How does that sound?" The little kids were clapping.

Great, Cheryl thought. How in the world can I eat that hard stuff? She's probably doing it to be mean because she knows I won't be able to eat it. Nonetheless, she pushed away from the table and got the cookie sheet out to toast the bread. At least the little kids got something out of her ordeal.

"Cheryl, while you're at it, make another pot of coffee. I need some to top off my breakfast."

"Be sure to measure the grounds better this time. It was too strong on the first pot." This was Daddy's comment on the breakfast.

Mama and Daddy left the kitchen with the little kids enjoying their Sunday treat of cinnamon toast. Cheryl rinsed out the old coffee grounds and carefully measured out more for fresh coffee. She filled the pot with water and plugged it in. Concerned about cleaning up the mess created by breakfast, she forgot to move the step stool from next to the sink by the coffeepot. Suddenly she heard a loud crash. Whirling around, she saw Eddie tangled in the coffeepot cord, hanging off the step stool. Watery coffee and coffee grounds were all over the cabinets, the floor, and Eddie.

Mama and Daddy rushed in. "What's going on in here?!" As if playing "freeze tag," all the children suspended their action and stood stock-still. "Can't you kids behave for five minutes?" Mama was building up. Her voice was getting louder and louder. She was shaking her fists at the kids and stomping her foot. The veins in her throat and on her forehead were bulging out. Crimson color rose from her chest, up her neck, and then spread over her face. She twisted her mouth and face. It was very frightening. This was always the prelude to a terrible beating of some or all of the children. Bea was chasing Cheryl around the table, hitting her randomly whenever she got close enough.

Renny scooped up Davey, Richie and Kati, tossed them into the bedroom, and closed the door. Satisfied that Cheryl knew she'd failed in watching the smaller children, Bea ceased chasing and hitting her.

Eddie was about three and a half years old at the time. Though

Davey was older, Eddie was taller than him and almost as tall as his older sister. He was disturbingly thin. Without a shirt it was easy to see that his rib cage was clearly defined. Eddie was constantly losing his pants because he was so thin. He still got Davey's hand-me-downs, which were a few inches too short for him.

Someone had given Eddie an old pair of cowboy boots that he proudly clomped around in. He wore those boots with long pants, short pants, or even with his underwear only. Sometimes he even slept in them. His hair was cut in a short crew cut. The color was medium brown, a mixture of his father's fair blonde hair and his mother's almost black hair. He did have his mother's flashing, shiny black/brown eyes. They were glistening now with fear. Eddie almost always had his left hand at the waistband of his pants, sort of a convenient "built-in" belt.

Though very young, Eddie had early on become acquainted with pain and suffering. He learned to conceal his emotions, finding that Bea and Renny often overlooked him in their rages because he stayed physically and emotionally lethargic. It frustrated his parents that Eddie seemed so apathetic. Today it made them angry. "Eddie, I think it's time for the bag game." Renny was menacingly edging toward him. Eddie resisted the impulse to run.

Effortlessly, with no struggle or resistance from Eddie, Renny placed him in a large plastic bag. Eddie drew himself into a solitary embrace, hugging his knees to his chest, squeezed his eyes closed, and waited like Cheryl for "The Black" to carry him away from his agony. First came the suffocating heat and sweat, then the alarm of his lungs starving for oxygen, the pounding in his head and then, thankfully, "The Black." Eddie had conquered the fear that used to consume him. He knew that once in the plastic sack for a while, "The Black" always carried him away.

Once "The Black" took over he would see a tunnel and light. Eddie knew it was Jesus. Eddie liked Jesus. He knew he was supposed to like God too, but God scared him. God was bigger than Daddy. Pictures of Jesus soothed him and gave him a sense of calm. Inside the plastic bag, with the help of "The Black," Eddie hoped to be able to reach Jesus and escape the misery he was continually forced to endure.

Suddenly, Eddie felt his chest heave and his head erupt with pain as oxygen burst through his system. Bea dumped him out of the bag and Eddie exploded back into the existence he knew as life. Cheryl wordlessly took his hand and helped him onto the bed where he would lie until sleep carried him away from the terrible headache. She gently stroked his back until he fell asleep, then she carefully tiptoed from the room.

FIVE

THE FAMILY BACKGROUND

That Sunday was the last for several years that the Morgan family would spend together. In the early morning hours on Monday a sharp knocking sound awakened the sleeping household. Renny stumbled out of bed and peered out through the curtains. He could distinguish shadowy figures moving stealthily around the house. Toward the street he saw police cars lining up. Shocked and nearly petrified, Renny shook Bea. "Bea... Bea, I don't know what they're here for, but it's the police. They're everywhere! What can we do?" The persistent pounding at the front door interrupted them.

"Open up! Police!" The pounding continued. Renny crammed his bare feet into his shoes and answered the door.

"Mr. Morgan, you are under arrest for..." Renny's head reeled as they read a long list of charges. "Do you understand your rights?" Renny desperately wanted to run, to escape somehow. He had too much weight on him. There was Bea, who was pregnant again, and Cheryl, Davey, Eddie, Richie and Kati. The officers were frisking him; the one in front of him demanded again, "Mr. Morgan, do you understand your rights?"

"Yes, sir." Renny could hear Bea crying. He would have to call his dad. Hank would bail him out. He turned to Bea, "Don't worry, honey. I'll call Dad. He'll take care of everything." They were handcuffing him now and guiding him out the door. He turned, his hands shackled behind him.

Bea was hovering, crying in their bedroom doorway, the three little boys clinging to her legs. In another doorway stood Cheryl with Kati on her hip. All the children were frightened and crying. Renny was ashamed for them to see him like this. He choked back tears and fought the fear constricting his throat. Turning quickly, he ducked his head down as they placed him in a squad car. Renny thought as they pulled away that it was amazing how silent and peaceful the house looked from the outside that night.

He relaxed a little as they pulled away. Hank would take care of whatever the charges were against him. Ole' Dad had always come through before. It might be a little awkward for Renny to call him since they'd had no contact for a while. Renny had no doubt, though, that Hank would send whatever money he needed, without delay, to keep Renny out of prison. He was only a phone call away from freedom.

* * *

Bea had no other choice except to load up the children and drive back to South Dakota. She and the children settled into a Quonset hut duplex subsidized by the government. ADC (Aid for Dependent Children) helped Bea with the financial responsibility of five children and doctor bills for the sixth child soon to arrive.

Though surrounded by all her children, Bea felt very much alone. She longed for Renny but had reconciled herself to the reality that it would be a minimum of three years before he could be released from prison.

She'd never had friendships, so she welcomed the friendship of Shirley the woman occupying the other side of the duplex. Shirley was married and had two little girls, two and three years old. She was married to a semi truck driver nicknamed "Brownie" who was often gone on cross-country runs. The adults would play cards at Shirley's.

Brownie would pay Cheryl a quarter to watch all the children on Bea's side of the duplex. It gave Cheryl a rare sense of importance to be entrusted with all the children. Brownie would always pat Cheryl on the shoulder as he left his girls with her and say, "I believe you'll take good care of my girls, Cheryl, because you're a good girl." Cheryl adored Brownie. The feeling was mutual according to conversations Cheryl overheard between Bea and Shirley. Bea often said, "Brownie thinks the world of Cheryl." Shirley would always agree, "He'd cut off his right arm for her." It worried Cheryl that Brownie might have to cut off his right arm for her.

Bea had another friend named Carol who had had a stroke and lost the use of her right arm. It just lay in her lap all the time. She could still play the piano one handed and sounded just about as good as a two-handed person. If Brownie cut off his right arm, he could probably still drive a truck one-handed, Cheryl thought. Carol did all right with one arm, and she wasn't nearly as big or as strong as Brownie. Cheryl was always very cautious around Brownie hoping she never did anything that might cause him to have to cut off his right arm for her.

The days and weekends passed and Bea's stomach was enormously swollen with the pregnancy. Carol came over one afternoon and Bea chased all the children outside, trusting them to Cheryl's watchful eye. The children knew that when Carol and Mama chased them out so they could talk, it would be a long time before they'd be allowed back inside.

Sitting lined up on the curb, Cheryl could hear music in the distance. Jumping up she exclaimed, "It's the carnival! Brownie told me there was a carnival coming to town!" She pulled Davey to his feet. "Run in and ask Mama if I can take all the kids downtown to watch the carnival set up. Hurry!"

Davey sprang up quickly but then timidly approached the front door. With encouragement from the children he finally dared to push the screen door and venture inside. In an amazingly brief time, Davey emerged from the house shaking his head in the affirmative. Cheryl and the other children were elated.

Cheryl was to find out shortly that Davey hadn't even dared to ask Bea's permission. He also didn't risk telling his older sister "no." He'd been on the receiving end of her anger also.

Cheryl had Davey, Eddie, and Richie take hands as she hitched Kati up on her hip, and off they went to the carnival. What a wonderful sight! A carousel, Ferris wheel, bumper cars – so much music and activity! The children were so excited that Cheryl had difficulty keeping up with all of them, darting in and out of all the confusing maze of people, workers, cables and booths. Suddenly Cheryl heard someone calling her name.

Pivoting around, she was delighted to see Mrs. Johnson, her

Sunday school teacher. Mrs. Johnson quizzed Cheryl about being at the carnival alone, and then kindly offered them a ride home. The boys were so enthralled with the carousel horses that Mrs. Johnson asked Cheryl, "Have you children ever ridden a carousel?"

"No, ma'am."

"Here," Mrs. Johnson said, opening her purse, "let's buy tickets and ride the carousel. It's a shame to come to a carnival and not get to ride anything before you go home." With that they all jumped on the ride.

Cheryl liked Mrs. Johnson. She had reddish hair and always wore white gloves on Sunday. Her purse was always the same color as her shoes. When I grow up, Cheryl thought, I'll be rich and have matching shoes and purses in every color of the rainbow.

Mrs. Johnson had taught the Sunday school class about the rainbow, God's seal on His promise that no flood would ever again cover the earth. Cheryl and Davey especially were glad to hear this story because Renny or Bea would often take them and hold them under water in the bathtub if they were really bad. It made their chests hurt inside. They would be plunged into icy water, sometimes after being jerked up out of a sound sleep.

Mama and Daddy were both very strong. No matter how hard Cheryl and Davey struggled and kicked, they'd force them to stay under the water. When they did let the children up it was to scream at them. Cheryl and Davey were unable to comprehend what they were being asked or screamed at for.

When they were finally brought up from under the water, they would so desperately gasp for air that nothing else mattered.

Thankfully, Renny and Bea usually tired of the "icy water game" pretty quickly. With pounding hearts, screaming lungs, heaving chests, freezing cold and thus terrorized, the children would climb into bed to comfort and warm each other.

If that was what a flood was like, no one would want to have that happen ever again. Cheryl felt peaceful whenever she saw a rainbow. Perhaps it was a special message from God that someday they wouldn't have to endure their own private floods.

Mrs. Johnson also said that Jesus was everywhere all at the same time. She said if you would just ask Him to help you if you were scared or hurt, He would. Cheryl knew with all the hurting kids there must be in the world, Jesus must surely be busy. She figured that sometime, though, He would help her if things got really bad.

It was wonderful to have hope of some protection and comfort and safety. It was like a secret treasure knowing she had Jesus to ask for help. She didn't know how many times He would help, though. She didn't want to risk using up all her chances and then need help on something really bad, and Jesus would say, "Sorry, you ran out of lucky tickets that let Me help you." She was going to save up and wait until she just couldn't take it anymore, then she'd ask for help. But Jesus would have to understand that she couldn't leave the rest of the kids. He'd have to help all of them, too. The way Mrs. Johnson explained it, though, Jesus was pretty big and had a pretty big place in heaven, and so it shouldn't be a problem for Him.

The carousel stopped and the excited kids hopped off and climbed into Mrs. Johnson's car. Cheryl had a sense of impending doom. She knew that Mrs. Johnson wouldn't let them out at the corner; she'd insist on coming to the door with them. If Carol was still there it might be okay. If she was gone, it was going to be awful.

Mrs. Johnson knocked and Cheryl and the kids came spilling in the door. Mama was in the recliner chair and rose up, startled at their entrance. She saw Mrs. Johnson looming in the doorway and stumbled up hurriedly trying to gather up the romance magazines lying around. She tried to casually kick dishes, cups and silverware strewn on the floor under the edge of the sofa as she worked to exchange pleasantries with Mrs. Johnson.

Mrs. Johnson pretended not to notice. She chuckled as she told Bea about the children's escapade at the carnival. Bea was horribly embarrassed to be caught seemingly neglecting her children. She was vaguely apprehensive about the welfare worker finding out about this. It was a small town. There was a strong possibility word of Cheryl's little adventure would reach Renny's parents. It would give Anna Morgan just the ammunition she needed to try to take the kids away again.

Years earlier the elder Mrs. Morgan had seen the deplorable conditions that the children lived in, and she had the welfare department visit her son and daughter-in-law's home. Renny and Bea left West Virginia and began moving from state to state to avoid further investigation and to escape Renny's mother's criticism. After Renny was arrested in New Mexico, Bea had no resources and had to accept the Morgan's help. Though they were now living in South Dakota, Bea couldn't risk having another encounter with the welfare department over her lack of parenting and household skills.

Once she was able to gracefully get rid of Mrs. Johnson, Cheryl was going to pay dearly for this. Bea deliberately kept her voice level, light, and low pitched. She was aware of the frozen smile on her face. This prim little church woman was going on and on. Bea was desperate to get her out of the house. She thanked her profusely and steered her determinedly toward the door.

Fear began to escalate in Cheryl as she listened to Mama talk to Mrs. Johnson. Recognizing the control in Mama's voice alerted her to the impending rage that would likely be directed at her. The other children sensed the anger in Mama lurking behind the fa-çade of the frozen smile. They nervously retreated out the back door and huddled in the tractor tire sand box. Cheryl felt a little relieved that Carol was still present. Mama usually didn't explode full force if an outsider was nearby.

Bea watched Mrs. Johnson's car disappear down the street, then turned slowly and deliberately toward Cheryl. She was very controlled, very much in authority, very aware of her power. She would have to teach her oldest daughter a lesson she'd never forget. Bea's mother, Mary Cutter, had always declared, "A child doesn't learn a lesson unless you draw blood." Bea understood what she meant now that she had children of her own.

"Cheryl, go into my room. Get two of Daddy's belts and go into the bedroom and get ready for the whipping of your life." Bea kept her voice low and calm. She had to let Carol know she was in charge of these children. She understood how difficult it was rais-ing children alone. She'd show Carol that Cheryl was not going to get out of control like Carol's children had. Bea turned toward the bedroom, graciously excusing herself as she called to Carol, "This will take a little bit. Help yourself to some more coffee. I'll be back in a few minutes."

Bea's heart was pulsating persistently in her throat as she closed the bedroom door behind her. She shoved Cheryl against the wall. Grabbing Cheryl's throat, she pounded her head against the wall, "Why do you do this to me? What is the matter with you?" Her voice was escalating in pitch. She deliberately kept the volume low. The energy it took Bea to refrain from her usual screaming rampages seemed to infuriate her all the more.

"Don't you know that you could be the cause of my losing all your brothers and your sister Kati?" Bea dropped her to the floor in disgust. Cheryl curled up in a ball on the floor. Bea was enraged to see her acting so childish.

"Get up!" Bea lost control and was screaming now. "Stand up! Get over here by me! Quit being such a baby. You're almost six years old. Don't you care about anybody but yourself? How did I ever end up with such a stupid, selfish, inconsiderate brat as you?"

Bea realized she needed to quiet down because Carol might hear her. She grabbed Cheryl by the back of her hair and drew her close so they were nose to nose. Through gritted teeth Bea spat her wrath into Cheryl's pinched and frightened face. "You disgust me. It is revolting to me to even look at you." Bea could see the terror in Cheryl's eyes. It seemed her eye sockets were vibrating with fear.

It gave Bea considerable satisfaction that she was making her point. Sometimes she wondered if the children were getting so toughened to her discipline that it didn't even faze them anymore. Well, this would be one whipping Cheryl wouldn't soon forget. "Lay across the bed," she demanded. Cheryl was whimpering now. She hadn't dared to cry out. "I'm going to draw blood this time, Cheryl, and Carol is here, so we can't make too much noise. Stuff this diaper in your mouth."

Cheryl clutched her legs and pleaded, "Please, Mama, please don't. I promise I won't ever do it again." Cheryl was desperate. She almost revealed to Mama that Davey had lied about Mama's permission. She couldn't do that. Mama stood looking at her. It seemed she was wavering. Cheryl begged one more time.

Falling to the floor and clutching her mother's legs, she implored, "Mama, I love you. I learned my lesson. I won't take the kids anywhere again. Please don't."

Mama was raising the belts. Cheryl tried again, "Okay, okay, just hit me a few times. Okay, twenty lashes. Please don't make me bleed!"

Bea considered, "I don't know, Cheryl, if I relinquish this time and give you a light whipping, I know I'll just end up doing it several times. This way I know it will last a longer time."

Mama was calming down. Cheryl was hopeful. "You don't want Carol to see you hitting me really bad, do you?"

It was the wrong thing to say. Bea sent Cheryl sprawling across the room. "Get that diaper in your mouth!" Cheryl obediently stuffed the diaper in her mouth. She was already crying. Bea could tell Cheryl was going to be difficult. Bea started crying, too. "Damn, you kids. I work hard trying to raise you and this is the thanks I get. So you think I'll be embarrassed because somebody's here? Wrong, young lady! Wrong! Wrong! Wrong! I can do whatever I want. The law gives me that right. You want to call the police? You go right ahead. They can come and take all you brats away. I never want to see you again. Oh, you think you'd like that, don't you?"

Cheryl was violently shaking her head no. Bea took another diaper and tied it so the gag would stay in place. She kept shrieking at Cheryl as she tied her wrists above her head to the bedpost. "You just go ahead and call the police. They'll take you all away. Oh, you won't see me again, or Daddy. But you won't see Davey, or Eddie, or Richie, or Kati ever again. How would you like that? Never again see them, Cheryl. Never. You'll all go to live in different homes with mean people who will never let you outside; never let you see each other, never feed you anything but bread and water. Is that what you want? Answer me! Is that what you want?" Cheryl frantically shook her head "no."

Bea took up the belts and with the buckle end began hitting Cheryl all over, again and again. Mercifully, Cheryl passed out before Bea's anger was spent. When no one else came to help, "The Black" was always there for escape.

* * *

When Cheryl awakened, the house was dark and quiet, hot and stuffy. She was curled up on the wood floor in a fetal position. Her mouth was dry, from the diaper she supposed. Apparently, Mama had untied her wrists and the gag. As she sat up and slowly straightened, the shirt she was wearing began pulling away from her back, like pulling adhesive tape off a wound where the blood had dried.

71

The saltiness of the sweat trickles as they made their way down her back stung in the open wounds on her shoulders, back and legs. She raised her hot, swollen and bruised face to the window. There were streaks of light coming through the window. It was dusk and she could see little dust particles swirling lazily in the light. It looked like heaven reaching down toward her.

This was a time she could use up a request for help from Jesus. "Jesus," she prayed, "I know You can't kill me because You are good, but please forgive me while I pray to the devil and ask him to kill me so I can die and come live with You."

In that moment of desperately crying out, Cheryl felt Jesus enfold her tiny, bruised body in His arms. It seemed He drew the pain out of her aching body, the sting out of her wounds. She felt a coolness come over her hot, swollen face and body, like He was gently blowing away the bad. A peace settled over her like she'd never known before.

Hope welled up within her. For the first time in her almost six years of life, she felt real hope, and love. She felt like a child instead of an old person trapped inside a child.

Cheryl knew she'd used up one of her allotted opportunities for Jesus to help her, but she didn't mind. Years and years later she would recall that moment of the enfolding love she felt that day. The reality of that moment of total peace, safety and love would never fade with the passing of time. Those few moments were a link in the chain of experiences that provided the vital connection for Cheryl to endure, to grow up, and become a survivor of abuse.

SIX

Not long after the circus incident, Bea would need the help of Mrs. Johnson as she was about to give birth to her sixth child. She had called for her to stay with the children as she went into labor during the night and was taken to the hospital.

Mrs. Johnson had already scrubbed each child, scoured the cabinets, sterilized bottles, washed mounds of dishes, and had a good start on the heaps of dirty laundry strewn all over the house. The children had awakened to the smell of sausage and pancakes. They enjoyed eating their fill with the added bliss of a warm, peaceful atmosphere. The kitchen was filled with a rare sound, the laughter and happy sounds of children savoring a good meal seasoned with silly, childish dialogue.

It was almost lunch when Mama telephoned. Snow was cascading down outside so all the children were in, close by, waiting for Mama's call. All five Morgan children crowded around Mrs. Johnson as she talked on the telephone. Mrs. Johnson had told them to pray for Mama. She said the doctor had told Mama that the new baby inside her tummy didn't have a heartbeat. The children all knelt by the sofa with Mrs. Johnson and prayed for the baby and Mama.

Cheryl and Kati wanted a sister to even out the Morgan family ratio of boys to girls. Mama had said she would name a girl Karoline Lynda -- Karoline to match Katrina (Kati's real name) and Lynda to match Cheryl's middle name. If it was a boy she was going to name him Gregory Nathan. "Gregory" because she liked the name, and "Nathan" because that was her father's name. Even though she'd never met her father, Bea talked about him sometimes. She told Cheryl it made her feel "connected" to him to talk about him.

Now Cheryl anxiously studied Mrs. Johnson's face as she talked with Mama on the telephone. Detecting no sadness, Cheryl relaxed a little. Finally, Mrs. Johnson handed the receiver down to Cheryl.

"Mama, Mama, is the baby born?" Cheryl was smiling as the other children jumped up and down.

The children were ecstatic and had to interrupt. "What is it, what is it? Is it a boy or a girl? Come on, Cheryl, tell us!"

Cheryl hugged the receiver to her chest, jumping up and down, "It's a girl! It's a girl!"

Positioning the phone so she could continue her conversation with her mother, Cheryl listened to Mama talk about the baby.

"Guess what her name is?" Mama said.

"Karoline Lynda!" Cheryl was smug; she was sure she had the right answer.

"No. Try again." Mama sounded happy.

"Not Gregory Nathan for a girl!?"

"No, Cheryl, I gave her a special name. The doctor told me last night that the baby didn't have a heartbeat and that it would be stillborn. That made me really sad because I didn't want this baby to die. I started reading the Bible. I read the 23rd Psalm and it helped me, so I kept on reading. I stopped at a verse that talked about weeping for a night, but joy coming in the morning. It was like a special message from God. Then this morning when the baby was born and she was all right, I remembered that verse. So, I decided to name the baby Karoline Joy."

"I think that sounds pretty. Are we going to call her Karoline or Joy?" Cheryl asked.

"I think we'll call her Kari. That way her name will match Kati's. She looks just like Kati. Her hair is almost snow white -- the little bit that she has -- and she has big blue eyes. People might think they're twins when they get older."

* * *

Mama had always wanted identical twins. She was disappointed that Cheryl and Kati didn't look very much alike. Cheryl hoped the new baby girl would live up to Mama's expectations. She knew she disappointed Mama in how she looked, but Cheryl felt she could be a special friend, kind of a secret pal to Mama. She knew Mama was sad and lonely since Daddy was in prison. Sometimes she would sit on the floor by Mama's bed at night in the dark and listen to Mama tell her about her dreams for the future.

One time Mama had even raised up in the bed and looked at her lovingly. It was a wonderful moment. Mama said, "Cheryl, your face is covered over with the face of Jesus. I see Jesus' face instead of yours." Cheryl thought Mama was going to touch her face.

She instinctively reached up and touched her own face, almost expecting to feel a beard. She felt tingly inside, like she could feel all the blood swirling through her body, from the tips of her toes to the top of her head, and back through her heart. She closed her eyes, waiting for Mama's touch.

Mama broke the spell by saying, "Okay, I'm tired. Get out of here. Get back to bed." Cheryl often reflected about that night over the years and wondered if Mama had really seen Jesus' face instead of hers or if it had just been another one of Mama's weird games.

Daddy and Mama had gone to a missionary school for six weeks when Mama was pregnant with Cheryl. Mama told her they'd planned to be missionaries in South America. The missions school didn't like Mama though (according to Mama), and they made her do "menial tasks."

Cheryl wasn't sure what "meany all tasks" were, but it sounded pretty bad. Anyway, Mama said they kicked her and Daddy out of missions school because she refused to do "meany all tasks." Daddy had gotten pretty mad about it. He said they were against him because they found out he'd had a little trouble with the law.

According to Mama, Grandpa and Grandma Morgan had tried to get them back in because they'd paid for Renny and Bea's schooling, but it just didn't work out. Daddy said he wasn't going to ever go to church again because only "Hippocrits" (purposely misspelled here because that's what I thought the word was) "hippo-crits"went to church. Mama explained to Cheryl that (hypo-crites) were people who went to church just to show off how much better they were than others, and how much more money they had.

Mama said they liked to uncover "dirt" or "dirty laundry" (bad things about others) and be the first to expose it to the con-gregation, pretending it was a prayer request. Then, on every day except Sunday, they would be mean to people that weren't their friends. Daddy said, "They could have had all of me on the mis-sion field. Now they don't get any of me since they revoked my calling from me."

Cheryl pestered him until he finally explained that "revoking his calling" meant that they wouldn't let him do the job he believed God told him to do. Daddy thought his job was to be a missionary in South America. He was mad that they stopped him.

Cheryl wondered if Daddy really had wanted to be a mis-sionary in South America or if it was Grandma Morgan's idea. Cheryl was a keen listener to adult conversations and she knew that Grandma Morgan had fervently hoped one of her sons would become a minister so she could brag to her sisters about it.

She'd often heard her brag about her twin brothers that were ministers. Grandma Morgan held ministers in high regard. She'd also said she thought that Renny and Bea should have stopped having children after Cheryl. This didn't go over well with Cheryl because she loved all her brothers and sisters. Cheryl didn't blame Daddy for not wanting to go where hypocrites went to church. Sometimes Cheryl was fearful that Grandma Morgan might be a hypocrite. She couldn't be though – if Grandma Morgan couldn't get into heaven, nobody could.

Mama didn't like church either, but she liked some things about God. God was somebody even Mama was scared of. Mama had a list of things God didn't like, so Mama didn't do those things. Mama didn't smoke or drink or go to bars. She refused to be friends with anyone who was divorced. Mama also didn't say curse words in church. She said God would strike you dead with a lightning bolt if you cussed in church.

Davey and Cheryl wished someone would cuss in church so they could see if it was true. They did wonder, though, why a person didn't get struck dead for cussing other places. If God struck you dead for cussing at your kids, Mama would have been dead a long time ago, that's for sure!

Mama also thought God would be mad at her if she didn't keep the children in church. Every time they moved, Mama would find a church that had a bus to pick up children and she'd ship all the kids off to Sunday school. Since Daddy had gone to prison, Mama would go to church sometimes too. Cheryl figured she needed some grown-up friends. The children hadn't spotted any "hypocrites" at the churches they'd been to, but they kept an eye out for them.

Over the years church became a haven for Cheryl, Davey, Eddie, Richie, Kati, Kari and later their youngest sister, Rosie. Church was the one place they felt safe and secure. Even though they were aware many times that they were not as readily accepted as the clean, well-dressed children, they were grateful for the opportunity to be in church.

In church the Morgan children were touched by hands that

didn't seek to hurt them. They could sleep and doze in the pews and on the bus without fear of being ripped and jerked out of sleep to violence. They were fed little treats they didn't otherwise get -- candy, gum, popcorn, cookies and fruit.

Most of all, they got to experience the love of God and to see visible glimpses of hope, of peaceful lives, of loving families, of people to look up to and to say, "Someday I'm gonna be just like him, or just like her."

They found comfort and reassurance in replaying for each other the Bible stories they heard and singing the familiar songs. The children had incredible memories for words and knew all the verses of songs that were four and five verses long. "Victory in Jesus," "When The Role is Called Up Yonder," "Trust and Obey," "There Is Power In The Blood," and "Love Lifted Me" were some of their favorites.

Their very favorite game was to "play church." Davey was always the preacher, Eddie was the offering taker, and Richie was the special music. Cheryl played the preacher's wife, standing beside Davey, smiling and shaking hands and "amen-ing" everything "Brother Davey" preached. Kati and Kari were always the preacher's children, the ones everyone wanted to hold and tickle and pass back and forth.

* * *

"Well, I'm tired," Mama's voice interrupted Cheryl's thoughts. "Give the phone back to Mrs. Johnson. You make sure all the kids behave and you help Mrs. Johnson."

"I will, Mama." Cheryl promised.

By the time Bea arrived home with baby Kari, Mrs. Johnson had the children and the house spic and span. The children lay stiffly in the bed as Mrs. Johnson read a bedtime story and tucked them in. It was very uncomfortable for all five children because they didn't know what to expect from her. They liked Mrs. Johnson, but they were leery. Silently they watched as she worked about the house. They spoke in hushed tones and moved self-consciously past her.

At mealtime they found it staggering to see how much food she prepared for them. Cheryl fretted over what Mama would say about the missing groceries. Luckily, Mrs. Johnson had brought some of her own food over. The boys were getting use to her. Mrs. Johnson was a "head patter." At first when she extended her hand toward them, they would dodge her and hit the floor. When they learned she was not intending to strike them, they began to bow their heads to receive her gentle caress. It had been a fun, carefree week for the Morgan children. Mrs. Johnson would certainly be missed. It was amazing that she had not blown up one time.

Now, Mama was coming in the front door. They'd missed Mama too, and were glad to see her come home. Everyone was anxious to see their new little baby sister, Kari. They crowded around as Bea, smiling proudly, lifted the soft pink hospital blanket from little Kari's face.

* * *

The tiny "tin" house with two bedrooms and six children soon proved too small for the Morgan family. Just before school started, Hank and Anna Morgan helped Bea settle into an old, two-story frame house about an hour's drive from them. The children were delighted with the upstairs. The climb itself was an adventure. The whole upstairs was one big open room. Bea put two mattresses on the floor and designated the upstairs the big kids' room. This meant that Cheryl, who had just turned eight, Davey, seven years old, Eddie, six, and Richie, five, shared the upstairs.

Kati, now almost four, and Kari, two, shared one downstairs bedroom, and Bea had her own room. Bea often said, "I can't ever get away from you blasted kids except in my room. No one is ever allowed in my room." That was fine with the kids most of the time. Bea was a big grouch if they woke her up before she was ready. She liked to take long naps, too. When Bea was taking her nerve pills she would take extra long naps. Cheryl and the boys would talk about "what if" Mama didn't wake up from one of her long naps someday. They all felt confident they could manage just fine without her.

Periodically the children would set out to make Mama laugh and have fun. Sometimes she would allow herself to play with them. It was curious because she would abruptly stop, as if suddenly reminded that she was to abstain from pleasure.

There were times that Bea would sit and tell the children stories of when she was a little girl. She usually got in a story-telling mood when she took a little extra nerve medicine. The children felt sorry for Mama because her mama had been very mean to her.

Cheryl wanted to reach out and comfort her mother, but Bea resisted loving contact from her children. She tried desperately with her eyes to communicate to Mama that she loved her and was sorry for how mean Grandma Cutter had been to her. Bea misinterpreted Cheryl's gaze and punished her soundly for glaring. All the children learned to keep their heads lowered in Mama's presence and to avoid direct eye contact with her whenever possible.

Sometimes Mama would have a friend over for the night. She made Cheryl take all the children upstairs for the night, even Kati and Kari. Mama said there were rats in the house at night. If children didn't stay in their beds at night the rats would come and rip their jugular veins out of their throats and Mama would find six bloody, dead children in the morning. The younger children were very afraid, but Cheryl had her doubts. Nonetheless, she lay with a blanket pulled up to her chin at night to keep her jugular vein protected.

One night Cheryl heard Mama and a man talking and laughing downstairs. Curiosity won out over fear and Cheryl rolled off the mattress. In a sitting position she ventured down the steep stairs, lowering herself one step at a time. About halfway down she saw something glistening on the stair in front of her. She sat paralyzed a few seconds until her eyes adjusted. Immediately she realized it was the "phantom rat" Mama had warned about – but this one was real.

Thankfully, Cheryl had dragged one of Kari's blankets with her. She crammed it into her mouth to muffle the terrified scream that intensified as she backed up the staircase. The rat never moved. Cheryl lunged onto the mattress, and wrapping the baby blanket around her throat, she pulled all the other children in close around her, making sure they were covered also to their chins. Daring not to close her eyes, Cheryl lay in wait for the rat. Finally, the early light of dawn pacified her enough that she reluctantly succumbed to sleep.

Bea's shrill shrieking awakened all the children more effectively than any obnoxious alarm. They all hurried to the top of the stairs. Bea was standing on the fifth step up. Several steps up from her, in the middle of the stairwell, caught in a trap was Cheryl's rat. No wonder he hadn't chased after her. Mama's friend came up the steps, and like a gallant hero, transported the rat from the staircase to the garbage. Cheryl secretly wished the rat would bite Mama's friend in the jugular vein.

SEVEN

The house was filled with the aroma of chocolate. Standing on a chair, using her skirt as a potholder, Cheryl was briskly stirring a batch of fudge. Mama was hurrying to get it ready. Grandpa Morgan would be by soon to pick it up. This was visiting day at the prison and Grandpa had a long drive ahead of him. Mama never went to visit Daddy. She said that it embarrassed him for her to see him like that, and it made her very sad. She sent him letters often and sent fudge with Grandpa Morgan on visiting days.

Cheryl wished Grandpa Morgan would hurry up. It was almost time for her and the boys to leave for school. Grandpa always had a jelly jar of pennies with him. He would entrust them to Cheryl to divide out equally among the children. On his way home from visiting Renny, Grandpa would take them to the dime store to spend their pennies.

Cheryl felt a tugging on her skirt. It was Kati, wanting her attention. As she turned, she knocked the cup of milk out of Kati's hand. Instinctively reaching down to help, Cheryl forgot her skirt was wrapped around the stirring spoon for the fudge. Boiling chocolate spattered all over the kitchen, some of it dropping on Cheryl and Kati's skin. Both cried out as the boiling liquid burned them. Mama, running into the kitchen, exploded with rage. She jerked both little girls by the hair and started swinging wildly at them with the poker beside the corncob stove.

She nicked Kati on the ear with the poker. Kati howled and ran, out of control, berserk with pain and terror. Bea pursued Kati, forgetting about Cheryl for the moment. Just as she caught her and was battering Kati's head against the wall, the boys shouted from the kitchen, "Gran'pa Morgan's here!" Bea let Kati tumble to the floor and dashed to the back door to meet him.

Cheryl rushed over to Kati on the floor. Picking her up and cradling her, she gently rocked her back and forth. Kati suddenly fell eerily silent. Almost as quickly as Kati had gotten so still, she began to twitch and jerk violently. She threw her head back and her eyes rolled way up into her head until all Cheryl could see was the white part of her eyes. Kati began clicking her tongue and sounded as if she were choking. Panicked, Cheryl yelled, "Mama, Mama! Something's wrong with Kati!"

Bea and Grandpa Morgan hurried into the kitchen to Kati and Cheryl. "Oh, my God! It's a convulsion – a seizure!" Bea screamed, "Cheryl, run fast! Get a spoon! Kati's going to swallow her tongue! Hurry, or she'll die!"

Cheryl bolted over to the sink, snatched a spoon, and raced with it back to Mama. Mama grabbed the spoon and forced it into Kati's mouth and held it there until the spasms in Kati's little body subsided. Suddenly Kati appeared to be asleep. Cheryl was afraid.

"Mama, is she dead?"

"No, stupid, she's not dead; she's asleep. You're going to have to watch the kids while Grandpa Morgan and I take Kati to the hospital. It's another convulsion from her epilepsy." Mama looked accusingly at Cheryl. "You shouldn't have scared her so bad, teasing her with that fire poker. Look, you've burned her and nicked her ear." Mama glared at Cheryl, daring her to defy her and contradict the story she was composing for Grandpa Morgan.

Cheryl was brighter than that. "Don't worry, Mama, I'll watch the kids. I'm sorry." Kari was pulling on Cheryl's skirt now. Reaching down, Cheryl hiked Kari up on her hip and retreated to finish the forgotten fudge. Mama hurried to prepare to leave for the hospital with Kati while Grandpa called Grandma Morgan to come stay with the other children.

Kati had five grand mal seizures that day. The eyestrain and other environmental factors in her life contributed to the gradual deterioration of her eyesight. Fitted with thick, tiny eyeglasses, Kati functioned from that point forward in a shadowy world with all detail forever obscured from her vision.

The damage of Kati's vision did effect a change in Bea. She controlled herself on "head banging" and never again banged the children's heads against the wall. Because of the epilepsy and Kati's poor eyesight, neither Renny nor Bea beat her again. This did not, however, prevent the other abuses Kati was subjected to. The other children grew to resent Kati because she was, in their eyes, favored because she wasn't beaten. They too subjected her to verbal abuse. Kati withdrew and encased herself into a defiant shell almost impossible to penetrate. Renny would get extremely enraged with

Kati because she would not give him the satisfaction of a response. He would call her names, push her, kick her, pull her hair, twist her arms, and still he would get no reaction from her.

Kati would stubbornly set her jaw, tilt her chin in the air, and stare blankly into space. With her feet planted and arms crossed, in mute silence she endured whatever was done to her.

Cheryl would recall only two incidents that evoked a response from Kati. Renny had been very angry at Kati for not drying the dishes to suit him. He had hit her and screamed at her and gotten no reaction. In a moment of total uncontrolled anger, he backhanded her across the face so hard that he knocked her thick glasses off her face. Renny stomped over to where the fallen glasses lay and purposely stepped on them. One lens was crushed but not broken out of the frame. Kati, her jaw set, said in a gloating tone, "Now look. You'll have to buy me new glasses."

"By God, I won't. You can just wear them like this," Renny decreed. For almost two years Kati looked at the world through thick glasses, one side totally distorted by the splintered lens. Finally, Cheryl could stand it no longer. She spent afternoons going around town with a wagon collecting glass soda bottles. They could be sold for five cents each. After many, many trips with the wagon she finally had enough money to buy Kati some new glasses. Mama was impressed for once with Cheryl for sticking it out and saving up for the glasses, and she let her go to town with her and Kati to get the new lenses.

If there was one person Kati trusted, it was Cheryl. They had slept together since Kati had been born, and as the only two girls until Kari, they had been very close. Kati had expected to be glad for another sister when Kari was born, but found she resented her. Kari intruded on her close relationship with Cheryl. Still, Kati felt she had a special place in Cheryl's heart and she was constantly shadowing Cheryl wherever she went.

It was ironic that Cheryl was directly responsible for the second incident that penetrated Kati's protective shell and hurt her deeply. One day she was very angry with Kati because she was sitting idly daydreaming and humming while Cheryl worked furiously to accomplish a long list of tasks from Renny and Bea. It happened when Cheryl was almost twelve. She seized Kati by the shoulders and between gritted, clenched teeth, spat her anger and hatred at Kati. "I hate you, you spoiled little brat. I wish you'd never been born. When Mama was pregnant with you I wanted a sister, but now that I've got you it wasn't worth it. I wish you'd have died."

It was a few seconds in time that, for the rest of her life, Cheryl desperately wished she could retract and erase. Tears welled up in Kati's eyes and she shook involuntarily for a few moments before she regained control of her emotions. She spat in Cheryl's face and snarled, "I hate you too. I wish I was totally blind so I'd never have to see you again." She pushed past her sister and locked herself in the bathroom. Cheryl ran to the door crying, and banging on the door she shouted her anguish and remorse for her cruel speech. Kati was as mute and unyielding as the door she hid behind. Finally, Cheryl gave up and walked away.

Those two incidents hardened Kati more than ever. The obstruction of her physical vision was insignificant in comparison to how she blinded herself to any good or value in her perception of herself and others. It appeared Kati had resolved to live her entire life isolated from people and insulated from any emotion. She became so encased in silence that it seemed impossible anyone would ever penetrate past the walls she built. It appeared, much to Cheryl's regret, that she had forever destroyed her influence over Kati in that one moment of anger.

EIGHT

A gentle overnight snowfall had delicately blanketed the ground, turning the outdoors into a fairyland. Inside the Morgan household, innocence and ignorance veiled the ugly scars of poverty, filth and abuse. As the children grew they began to take note of the discrepancies between their existence and the lives of people around them. Christmas causes hope to flourish in the hearts and souls of adults and children alike, regardless of their outward circumstances. The Morgan children were no exception.

It was a clear, cold Saturday morning a few days before Christmas in South Dakota. Bea and Cheryl were busily bundling all the children for the journey across the street to the fire station. Santa Claus was scheduled to appear at 11:00 and hand out stockings full of candy to all the waiting boys and girls. Adorned with mismatched mittens, worn wooly scarves, oversized snow boots and charity hand-me-down snowsuits, all of Bea's children marched hand in hand out the door and across the street.

Patiently, with restrained excitement, the children waited in line for their turn on Santa's knee. When it came their turn, Cheryl ushered them one by one, according to age, up to Santa. Upon collecting their precious mesh stocking full of candy and a toy, she had them line up next to her and wait for the others.

First Kari, then Kati, Richie, Eddie and then Davey. With everyone clutching their stockings, Cheryl turned to direct them out the door. "Little girl," Santa called to Cheryl. She turned and he beckoned her to him. Reluctantly she approached his chair. "Honey, don't you want your turn with Santa?" He held out his arms to her.

Cheryl tiptoed up to him and leaned close so the littler children wouldn't hear. "No, I'm a big girl. I'm eight years old! I know you're not real, so I don't need to talk to you." She smiled at him and waved as she turned to go.

Santa beckoned her back to him. Leaning forward he said, in a very confidential tone, "I see that. I wonder if it'd be smart, though, for you to go ahead and take a stocking of candy anyway?" He winked at her, "The little children might not understand if you don't take a treat from me. They might wonder why I didn't give you anything, don't you think?"

She pondered that possibility then extended her hand for the stocking. "I'm sure you're right," she agreed, feeling very important indeed that he could recognize how grown up she was. With that, the six children marched home with their Christmas treats. At home they peeled off the layers of clothing and attacked the stockings full of candy. Each child selected some choice pieces of candy to present to Mama. They were excited to be able to give her something. Mama accepted their gifts of candy and put them in a bowl by her chair. She instructed Cheryl to keep the kids out of her candy while she went next door to visit her friend.

Mama's new friend was the neighbor named Paula. Paula had a husband, but the children almost never saw him. Paula's mother also lived with her. She was very old, probably about a hundred Cheryl guessed, and kind of sickly. Paula would pay Cheryl a dollar to come over and sit with her mother for the evening once a month while she and her husband went out.

Cheryl loved sitting with Paula's mother. It meant she had a whole dollar of her own. It meant she got away from all the kids and away from Mama. The most exciting benefit was that she got to watch television.

Paula's mother liked to watch the Red Skelton show. Before Cheryl saw the show for the first time she was scared. She was apprehensive that she would get frightened by the "red skeleton." Even though it sounded like a horror show, the kids at school would laugh about the red skeleton. Cheryl was too embarrassed to let anyone know they didn't have a television, so she just laughed with them.

No one she knew had a color television, so she figured a black and white "red skeleton" wouldn't be too scary. There was a boy named Andy whose father owned the furniture store in town. She'd heard his family had a color television. Cheryl was too shy to ask him if the skeleton on the show was really red. After she actually saw the show for the first time she was really glad she hadn't humiliated herself by asking anyone about the skeleton. Boy, would they have thought she was stupid!

Candy wrappers were everywhere. It was no use to try to

pick them up until the kids were through. Cheryl went to the little room off the kitchen to run a load of laundry through the wringer so she could hang them on the rack to dry in front of the oven. She was trying to straighten the house. A lady named Miss Ginny from the church was coming over .

She had asked Mama if Kati and Kari would be little angels in the Christmas pageant. They both had long, white-blonde hair. Kati's hair had never been cut and flowed almost to her waist. Kari had remained almost totally bald until she was a year and a half, but now suddenly her hair was almost to her shoulders in less than six months. It was thin and wispy, but she had little natural corkscrew curls that framed her tiny face.

Everyone said Kari looked like a little angel. It was a wonder anyone noticed their hair because all the Morgan children looked dirty and unkempt. It had also been said of them that they looked like little street urchins from a Charles Dickens novel. Miss Ginny had tactfully said she had some "special" shampoo for the girls; it would make their hair shine for the Christmas pageant. She had made some little angel costumes for them to wear. Miss Ginny was going to personally wash their hair so that it would be shiny and beautiful for the program.

Cheryl was singing a solo at the end of the program. She was going to play a poor little shepherd girl. She didn't really need a costume for that part; she could just wear her regular clothes – a dress that was really too big for her. Miss Ginny had promised that she would fix Cheryl's hair in an extra special way since she wouldn't get to wear a costume. The little boys were all going to be shepherds, and Miss Ginny was bringing terry cloth bathrobes for them to borrow. They had scrounged the yard and each selected a special stick to be their shepherd's staff.

As she squeezed the last of the laundry through the wringer, Cheryl paused to listen toward the living room. It was awfully quiet. She left the clothes halfway through the wringer and edged across the kitchen to the doorway. Cheryl gasped in horror at what she saw.

In the middle of the room, sitting cross-legged, side by side, were Kati and Kari. Standing above them was Richie, a pair of scissors held in his right hand, a long strand of blonde hair in the other. Accumulated in a gruesome circle around them was the rest of their beautiful hair. Kati's hair was cut to above her ears. Richie had cut off Kari's curls, one by one, missing only a few. The little tufted remains stood up in telltale patches all over her scalp.

"Oh, dear Lord, dear Lord." Cheryl held her face in her hands and rocked back and forth. "Richie, Mama's going to kill us both. We have to think of something quick." Cheryl felt desperately afraid.

Richie wasn't worried. "I'm going to be a barber when I grow up," he declared. "I was practicing. I'll make a lot of money and buy Mama lots of presents."

"I'll have to go over to Paula's and tell her. It'll be worse if she walks in on this. You'd better hide, Richie. I mean it," Cheryl warned the rest of the children. She ran out the back door and up the steps to Paula's back door. Mama and Paula were drinking coffee. "Mama, Mama, come quick," Cheryl had impulsively decided to play dumb. "Something bad has happened to Kati and Kari!"

Mama and Paula immediately lunged for the door and raced

across the yard. Cheryl caught up with them just as Mama saw the little girls standing proudly with their fresh haircuts in the middle of the evidence. Richie, unwisely, had not taken Cheryl's advice. He stood smiling proudly at his labor, the incriminating scissors still in his hand.

Mama was enraged. She hurled the scissors across the room and began screaming and punching Richie all around the room. Cheryl had never seen her this mad before. Mama's face was red. The tendons, muscles and veins in her neck and forehead bulged at the strain she was creating with her tantrum.

She got louder and louder, more and more angry. Perhaps embarrassed by Bea's anger, Paula retreated out the back door and slipped back home. When Bea heard the back door slam and realized Paula had left, she unleashed her anger in full force. Grabbing anything within reach she began hitting Richie over and over again.

Kari and Kati were screaming in terror and clutching Cheryl. Eddie listlessly observed while Davey retreated to a safe distance and continued to eat his candy as he watched. Finally, Cheryl could stand Richie's screams no longer and she risked interference. Running up to Bea, she yelled up at her, "Mama, stop. Richie's too little; he can't take it any more. I'll take his whipping." Bea paused a moment, shocked at Cheryl's boldness.

Quickly she regained her composure, "Don't you worry, little girl, you'll get yours. You were supposed to be watching them. What in the hell were you doing?" Bea focused her anger on Cheryl now. Cheryl knew it didn't matter to Mama what she was doing. She didn't waste her energy on arguing with Mama or defending

100

herself. She dropped her head and gaze toward the floor and waited for "The Black" to swallow her up as Mama hit her again and again.

When "The Black" lifted, Cheryl knew she hadn't been away long. She could hear Richie's screams and hear Mama still beating him in the other room. She covered her ears and squeezed her eyes shut, but she couldn't block out Richie's wailing, painful screams. She prayed Richie would just go ahead and die, or that "The Black" would come and mercifully swallow him up. Maybe one of God's lightning bolts would strike Mama so she would stop.

After an eternity to her childish mind, the screaming suddenly stopped and Mama emerged from the bedroom. She appeared limp and tired. Her shoulders were bowed. She dragged the belts along the floor, the buckles scraping as she walked. She was sweating and breathing hard. Cheryl knew Mama would withdraw to her bedroom now, probably for the rest of the day; take some of her nerve medicine and sleep.

After Mama closed her bedroom door, Cheryl waited until she was sure Mama was going to stay, and then she slipped into the bedroom to find Richie. He was curled up in a heap, moaning faintly under the bed. She coaxed him out and gently uncurled his body. Carefully she wrapped her arms around him and cradled him in her arms. She could feel the heat from the blows radiate from his entire body.

When his sobbing and moaning had eased, Cheryl tenderly peeled his shirt and pants off of him. She winced at the welts, bruises and blood blisters already formed. He had some raw and bleeding spots on his back, his bottom, and across his chest. The top of his legs had angry, smoldering red bruises with dark blood showing through just below the skin's thin surface.

Half carrying him to the bathroom, Cheryl wet a towel and gently wrapped it around his now sensitive shoulders and back. Next she wet two diapers and wrapped those around the tops of his legs. Carrying him back to the bedroom, she laid him across the bare mattress and then covered him with a blanket from the floor. Though Richie still hurt, he was too exhausted to cry anymore. He reached out, and with one small hand took hold of Cheryl's hand and comforted himself by sucking the thumb on his other hand.

Richie was already five and shouldn't be sucking his thumb, but Cheryl allowed it under the circumstances. She stroked his forehead until he fell asleep, then tiptoed out to find the other children.

What would Miss Ginny say when she saw the little hairless angels? She was probably going to be short one shepherd. Cheryl doubted that Richie would be out of bed for a few days. She knew from experience that it hurt too much to move for a day or two, then every extremity would get stiff, which made it even more difficult to move. The swelling and bruising would also increase with time, and some of the blood blisters would erupt into scabbed-over sores that sometimes took two or three weeks to heal over. Cheryl ached for poor little Richie.

"Someday," she vowed, "I'll get big and I'll get rich and I'll take care of the kids. I'll be nice to them and I'll feed them lots of food. I'll make sure they have new clothes to wear, not just hand-me-downs from other children that everyone knows were given to you. I'll take everybody to a real store and buy them a new pair of shoes -- shoes that no one has ever worn before. I'll buy Kati some real pretty eye glasses that are so good she'll be able to see clouds in the sky and birds in the air."

"For Kari I'll buy a real doll that's new, that's dressed, not naked, and one that doesn't have matted hair. I'll also buy her a new blanket so she can keep warm at night. For Richie I'll buy pants that fit and don't drag the ground, and I'll buy him suspenders and a belt. Cowboy boots, new from the store, with a matching belt is the first thing I'll buy for Eddie. For Davey I will have to buy a real tool box with tools in it so he can fix things."

Cheryl guessed she'd buy Mama a present, too. It would have to be some really pretty, sparkling jewelry. That's what Mama liked best. Oh, and she'd send Mama to the beauty shop. Mama loved going to the beauty shop. For herself, Cheryl would buy an Easter bonnet and white gloves. If she really had a lot of money she might also buy matching shoes and purses for Mama and herself and the two little girls. Of course, if she could do that she would also buy the boys a new shirt and a bow tie. They did have one bow tie. They took turns wearing it on Sundays. Cheryl kept track of whose turn it was to wear the tie. That prevented a lot of fights between the little boys.

For now, though, she'd be content for the throbbing in her back and legs to ease. Though it was really still too early for bed, the little kids didn't know it because it was dark outside. Mama had called Miss Ginny and told her to just come the next night - the night of the pageant. Cheryl made the kids get into bed quietly, warning them strongly not to disturb Richie. She settled into bed and prayed to Jesus, asking Him to please hold Richie and soothe him with the same peace and coolness and comfort she had experienced.

* * *

Kati and Kari sat perched on a little platform above the "manger" with a spotlight focused on them. Miss Ginny had fashioned "angel hair" for them out of silver tinsel with halos made of gold garland and a clothes hanger. The effect was glittery angels that sparkled in the magical Christmas lighting. The church Christmas tree was especially splendorous to the Morgan children because they didn't have a tree at home. It was marvelous just to watch the twinkly lights glowing in warm, colorful circles creating peaceful auras on the tree.

Sadly, little Richie was missing from the terrycloth-draped circle of shepherds with towels adorning their reverently bowed heads. The program was nearly over and Cheryl sat on the floor just out of view of the audience, leaning listlessly against the wall. The upset of Richie's battering two nights before and the physical effects of her own punishment along with the blame Cheryl took upon herself for Richie's pain had manifested itself in sickness. She had been vomiting all night and that Sunday, but she had insisted upon coming to the Christmas pageant. Miss Ginny had assured her that everyone would understand why she didn't sing her solo. She was determined, though, and Miss Ginny felt obligated to let her try.

Waves of nausea swept over Cheryl as she heard the introduction for her solo. As she stepped onto the platform and into the blinding light, she broke out into a cold sweat. It was not produced by nervousness but by turmoil. Bracing herself by planting her feet wide apart, and gripping the edge of the manger to further steady herself, Cheryl's fragile voice drifted across the church sanctuary.

"What shall I give Him, poor as I am..." Finally she came to the last line... "What shall I give... I'll give Him my heart." A hush had settled over the congregation. Cheryl's footsteps echoed loudly as she left the platform. She heard the congregation rise and burst out singing "Joy To The World." They did truly sound joyful as they sang.

Out of the spotlight, Cheryl relaxed and lay on the cool floor by the baptistery and closed her eyes. Sensing someone's presence, she looked up to see Mama watching her. Mama gently jostled her with a foot. "You did good, Cheryl. I was proud of you for going out there even though you were sick. Get up and let's get the little kids home. Richie is probably anxious for us to be back home." With some effort Cheryl lifted herself from the floor to follow Mama. Well, it had been worth it to sing even when hot, nauseated and dizzy. Mama was "proud of me." Cheryl felt a little better already. Mama was proud of her. That was a real Christmas miracle.

✳ ✳ ✳

Bea threw open the front door of their home and two little shepherds, two little angels and one street urchin paraded inside. Bea and all five children stood immobile as they stared at the scene before them. There, in the corner of the living room, stood Renny's brother, R.J., holding Richie. Behind him was a beautiful silver Christmas tree with wrapped presents underneath.

Off to the side, focused on the tree, was a light with a revolving color wheel attached. It made the silver tree change from silver to red to blue to gold to green as it rotated past the light. The children ran over to hug and climb all over Uncle R.J.

Uncle R.J. raised his voice above the excited voice of the children. "Mother and Dad couldn't make it, so they sent your Christmas with me." R.J. directed Bea to the kitchen where he showed her a box of groceries sent by Hank and Anna. Hank had had a heart attack a few weeks earlier and was still unable to travel. Anna, though having to "nurse" Hank twenty-four hours a day, had prepared a food box consisting of all the ingredients necessary to prepare a full traditional Christmas dinner. Anna had even made decorated Christmas cookies for the children and a box of fudge for Bea.

The children had followed them into the kitchen and were excitedly examining the groceries. Cheryl whispered to Davey, "See, I told you Grandpa and Granma Morgan were rich! Look at all this stuff!" Every time the family had visited their grandparents the children always found a full cookie jar. Cheryl had told the other children that this was clear evidence of wealth. They also had a stack of towels in the "linen" closet, and Grandma Morgan always had two sheets on each bed. This was also an obvious sign of affluence. The Morgan children usually slept on bare mattresses.

Richie was pulling on Uncle R.J.'s arm trying to head him back to the spectacular Christmas tree. Uncle R.J. (Richard James) acknowledged his namesake Richie, and allowed himself to be dragged back into the living room. He gestured toward Richie's visible bruises, asking Bea, "What happened to him?"

Bea flushed, thinking fast, "Oh, you know how clumsy Richie

is, and he's always tripping over his pants legs. He was climbing outside and fell out of a tree."

Thankfully, the children all clamoring for his attention distracted R.J. "Cheryl and Davey, since you two can already read, you pass out the presents. Once everyone has their presents, we'll watch each other unwrap," Uncle R.J. directed.

At last each child and Bea had two gifts apiece. The children were very excited. Uncle R.J. said, "Okay, let's unwrap them according to age. That means Kari gets to open hers first."

Little Kari didn't exactly understand what was going on but responded to the contagious excitement and happiness in the room. Her halo was lopsided now and the tinsel hair was reflecting the colors radiating from the color wheel. Curled up in Cheryl's lap, she buried her face bashfully as she realized all the attention was being focused on her.

"Come on, Kari, open your presents," Cheryl coaxed. With her sister's help, Kari unwrapped the first gift. It was pastel-colored terry cloth training pants from Grandpa and Grandma. Everyone was excited. Grandpa and Grandma always gave new underwear to the children for Christmas. It was wonderful to have something brand-new and store-bought to wear.

The second package was from Uncle R.J. Peeling back the paper from the odd-shaped package revealed a little, soft brown teddy bear. Kari's eyes widened, then she grabbed it. Holding it tightly tucked under her arm, she ran and scooted back into the corner behind the Christmas tree to watch everyone else. The children laughed at Kari's reaction.

Kati was almost four and knew she was next, so she started tearing the paper off her packages. The first was the expected package of new panties with delicate pastel flowers. Unashamedly, Kati stood up and immediately pulled on a pair. The others laughed, though embarrassed Kati had done that with Uncle R.J. watching. Kati ripped the remaining paper from R.J.'s present to her and squealed with pleasure at the Raggedy Ann doll inside. She too grabbed up her gifts and retreated under the tree beside Kari.

Richie, still sore, was sitting very still in Uncle R.J.'s lap, his head pressed against his uncle's chest. He was so enjoying the peace of being held that he declined opening his gifts. "I want to wait until last," he said as he nestled closer in Uncle R.J's embrace. "You're weird, Richie," said Eddie, lunging for his gifts. Inside the first package was the expected long underwear. "Long johns" they were called. The little boys were thankful for them. The nights got cold and the long johns helped them keep warm.

Now for the surprise from Uncle R.J. Inside were two boxes. One was a small heavy box of splendid ebony dominos. Eddie loved to play with a handful of black dominos he'd found. Now he had a whole box full of real dominos. The other box was kind of heavy also and it rattled. Opening it Eddie found a round metal checkerboard. On one side was a plain board for Chinese checkers and on the other a surface for regular checkers. Lifting the metal lid he found checkers and marbles stored inside. At six, Eddie was going to be "king" of the house when there was time to play games. "Thanks a lot, Uncle R.J.!" Eddie ran over and hugged him. From under the tree Kari and Kati echoed Eddie's thanks: "Thank you, Uncle R.J." "Thanks, Uncle R.J."

"Eddie, you be careful around Kari with those marbles. You wouldn't want her to choke on one, would you?" Uncle R.J. warned.

"No sir. I'll be careful," Eddie promised.

"Okay then, Davey," Uncle R.J.'s voice sounded so deep to the children, "it's your turn."

Davey quickly shredded the paper from both his gifts before he took time to look at either. Ripping the wrapping from the long johns, he held them up to assure himself they were long enough. Satisfied, he looked at his gift from Uncle R.J. "Oh, boy," he shouted. "It's Lincoln Logs! Thank you, Uncle R.J. Thanks a lot! I mean it! Thanks!"

Uncle R.J. looked pleased with himself for his success with such a delighted response from Davey. "Okay, Cheryl girl, it's your turn." Davey was almost as anxious as Cheryl to see what she'd received.

Being careful to save the lovely Christmas wrap, Cheryl opened the gift from Grandpa and Grandma Morgan. Inside she found pastel panties like Kati's without the floral pattern. Cheryl was glad because that would eliminate fights about which were hers and which were Kati's. True, Cheryl was eight and Kati was almost four, but they were all use to wearing ill-fitting garments, so Cheryl knew size wouldn't stop Kati from claiming her underwear. She was glad Grandma Morgan had thought of that.

Next she opened Uncle R.J.'s gift. Lifting the lid she gasped at the beauty of the gift inside. Laying in a soft nest of pink tissue paper lay a beautiful doll, glorious and resplendent in a full bridal gown, veil, and a rhinestone crown. Cheryl had never seen anything so beautiful. She ran to hug Uncle R.J. then rushed back to the box to admire the doll. She wouldn't ever take it out of the box. Those mean little boys might get the beautiful white wedding gown dirty. This doll was for display only. It was going to be her most treasured possession.

Bea too had gifts from the elder Morgans and Renny's brother. From the Morgans she received a warm flannel nightgown and from R.J., a flowered duster. Cheryl wondered why they called it a "duster." It was a robe that buttoned up the front. Bea wore them often. She sometimes called it a housecoat. Cheryl had never seen Bea dusting while wearing one, though. Probably in the olden days women wore them when they dusted and cleaned house. Bea never cleaned house. Any cleaning that got done was due to Cheryl's poor, untrained efforts. It made the house a challenge for visitors to tolerate for very long. R.J. was no exception.

"Well," he said, standing up and lowering Richie to the floor, "I have some gifts from Renny for everyone too." Opening a sack beside his chair he brought out some leather items. "Renny has been learning leather craft in the penitentiary. He's made a gift for each one of you. R.J. handed out the well-made, handcrafted leather items. For each of the boys was a leather belt with their names carved in the center of the back.

Kati and Kari were each handed a coin purse and a leather barrette. Cheryl watched Mama as Uncle R.J. handed the barrettes to the nearly hairless little girls. Mama didn't appear to react. Cheryl was handed her gift from Renny, a billfold with a place for pictures. Mama cried as she reached in the sack and pulled the last gift, an intricately designed leather shoulder bag. Inside was a matching billfold and attached to the strap, a matching key ring. "Tell Renny I miss him terribly the next time you see him," she said tearfully as she stood and embraced Uncle R.J.

"I will, Bea. I will," R.J. promised. "I'd better go now. I have a long drive back home."

"Wait, Uncle R.J., wait!" Cheryl yelled as she ran back to the kids' bedroom. Uncle R.J. had to have a gift from them. The only gift Cheryl had to offer was her still unopened mesh Christmas stocking. She ran, retrieved it, and rushed back down and presented it to Uncle R.J. "Here," she said, "this is your present. We've been saving it for you." Uncle R.J. lifted her up and gave her a squeeze. "Thanks, honey," he said, "I like it a lot. I don't have a Christmas stocking yet. It's just what I needed." Cheryl was proud of herself for thinking of such a perfect gift for her uncle.

Uncle R.J. felt someone tugging on his pant leg. "Uncle R.J.," it was Richie. He would turn five the first week in January. "I still have to open my presents."

"You're right, little man. Let's do it!" Richie happily tore the paper from his packages. "Look, I got long johns, too!" Cheryl and Davey shook their heads in disbelief, like it was a surprise – that's what Grandma and Grandpa Morgan always bought for the boys.

Next he opened Uncle R.J.'s gift. It was a bright red Tonka truck. Richie had two others that he played with, but they had no paint left on them, were missing wheels, and had dents. This was a brand new, shiny red truck with no dents and with all the wheels attached! Richie was very excited. "Thanks, Uncle R.J.!It's just what I wanted!"

All six children crowded in the open doorway, waving and calling their farewells to Uncle R.J. as they watched him drive away into the night. Mama was still clutching her new purse as she pushed the children away from the door and closed it. Cheryl noticed Mama still had tears in her eyes.

"I'm going to bed. You kids go, too. Cheryl, you turn out all the lights." Mama went to her room and shut the door. Opening it just a crack, Mama leaned out and said, "Since it's Christmas Eve you can leave the light on that shines on the Christmas tree. I think it will look pretty to wake up to."

"Okay, Mama, that's a good idea," Cheryl said. She was glad Mama had thought of it. She ventured to take advantage of Mama's Christmas charitable spirit. "Mama," she called. Bea peered out the crack of her bedroom door again. "Can we all sleep by the Christmas tree tonight?" Bea contemplated for a long moment. "I guess so, but you kids better keep quiet. That's an order."

"We will," Cheryl promised. Bea's door closed again. Cheryl and Davey dragged all the blankets to the tree and spread them out. They helped all the kids lay down and arranged the gifts so they were gathered around each proud new owner. After spreading the remaining covers over the children, Cheryl and Davey crawled under, too. The littler children quickly and peacefully fell asleep. Cheryl and Davey talked in hushed tones about Uncle R.J., Grandma and Grandpa Morgan, Renny and Bea, and Jesus.

Cheryl figured that when Renny got out of prison things would be better. Davey had his doubts. He still had distinct memories of Renny's kicking, stomping and choking methods of punishment. Cheryl assured him that Renny was being changed in prison. That's why the police sent people away who've been bad. They take them away and teach them how to be nice and how to treat everybody right. Davey still had his doubts. His daddy was a big, big man. He was skeptical that anyone would be big enough or strong enough to make Renny change. Cheryl assured him that Jesus could make anybody change.

She reminded Davey of what Miss Ginny had taught in Sunday school. Miss Ginny said that if "whosoever" (that included Renny) would ask to be "converted" (that meant changed for the better) that they would be "transformed" by Jesus, right away.

"Transformed" meant that any bad things about a person would change into good things. Once a person was "converted" they would act a lot like Jesus. That sounded like such a wonderful prospect that Cheryl and Davey knelt together beside the silver Christmas tree and prayed for Mama and Daddy to get "converted."

As they snuggled back down under the covers Cheryl felt very confident that Jesus had been listening to their prayer. It wouldn't be long now and they could be as happy every day as they were tonight. She closed her eyes and dreamed of a peaceful life, filled with happy moments, full cupboards, giving and receiving of gifts, no screaming, yelling, beatings and pain. Most of all, the whole family talking to and listening back to Jesus, together. "Someday, if they don't change, though, I'll grow up and save all of you," she silently promised her sleeping brothers and sisters.

NINE

It had been a glorious Christmas that year for the Morgan children, thanks to Hank and Anna Morgan and Renny's brother, R.J. Renny had also given, and all who saw it admired his fine leatherwork. Renny began sending pieces of leatherwork to Bea. She would then send the children out door to door to sell it for added income. They usually went out in teams of Cheryl and Davey or Cheryl and Eddie.

Richie wasn't allowed to go selling and he was impatient for the time when Bea would proclaim him old enough to sell door to door. Somehow Renny was also able to send other items to be sold: pens, earrings, and cufflink and tie bar sets. It soon became almost a daily event to "go out selling." Cheryl, Davey and Eddie always consoled Richie with the assurance that he was in reality "lucky" that he didn't have to go out selling. The three older children knew that they would not be allowed back home until they had sold the day's given quota.

One cold, rainy day Bea sent Cheryl out alone to sell. Davey and Eddie had been sick. Bea was not usually sympathetic to sickness, but the boys had run fevers with their colds and she wanted them well so they would be allowed to return to school. She was tired of having them underfoot all day without Cheryl to help.

Cheryl had to walk a long distance before she came to an area of town they hadn't covered lately. Already soaked and very cold, she knocked on door after door with no luck. Finally she was so cold and miserable that she determined it was worth it to go back home and risk a beating. Mama would always give them a choice when they returned home with no sales. They could either take a beating or go back out and try some more. Usually the children chose to go back out. It was during those times that they learned to put their prayers to practical use. They would pray together and then thankfully would usually make a sale that enabled them to return home.

Taking a shortcut through an alley, Cheryl stopped under the eave of a garage to shift her load. The sack was soggy and tearing. She was afraid it was going to burst open and ruin the merchandise inside. Taking off her sweater, she carefully removed the boxes of jewelry from the sack and transferred them to her sweater. The boxes were open with the lids on the bottom to easily display the jewelry inside.

Pulling the last box from the sack, she was alarmed to see that one cufflink was missing from the set. It was a tiger-eye cufflink. It would be hard to find on the dirt roads, even in daylight. It was already dusky as she hurried to retrace her steps back to the last house she'd shown the cufflinks to. She rapped impatiently on the door. The lady opened it, surprised to see Cheryl again. "Go home, little girl. I already told you. I don't need anything today."

"Wait, no, please," Cheryl stuck her foot in the door. "I can't find the other tiger-eye cufflink you looked at. Did I leave it here?"

"Honey, I don't know what you're trying to pull, but I don't have your cufflink. The lady started to push the door closed. Suddenly she seemed to really see Cheryl for the first time. "How old are you?"

"I'm eight and a half, almost nine."

"What's the matter with your mother? Does she know you're out here in this weather? Where's your coat? Don't you know the weatherman is predicting a blizzard tonight?" The lady towered high above Cheryl, questioning.

This could only mean trouble. Cheryl couldn't let her know her name. They might tell the welfare. Mama said if anybody said anything bad about her to the welfare, the police would separate them and they'd never see each other again. They fiercely protected each other and their mother from outsiders.

"Okay, sorry, thanks anyway," Cheryl called as she ran down the steps.

"Wait a minute," the lady called. Cheryl froze. "Stay right there. I'll be right back."

Oh, thank you, Jesus, thought Cheryl. She does have the cufflink. I can go home. She was immediately relieved. The lady walked briskly toward her. "Here," she said, "there's a sandwich and a cupcake in the bag for you. Let's put this dry cleaners bag over you to keep you from getting soaked to the bone." She tied a plastic rain bonnet on Cheryl's head. "You can keep the rain hat. Now, scram, run home before it starts to snow."

Cheryl was still shivering under the plastic but could feel some warmth creeping back into her body. "Thank you, lady. Thanks a lot," she called. Taking painstakingly small steps, Cheryl again retraced her path since leaving the lady's house the first time. Her eyes darted back and forth carefully inspecting the ground for any sign of the missing cufflink.

Too quickly she again reached the spot where she had discovered her loss. She took off her shoe and emptied the change inside. People who didn't buy often gave her a nickel or a dime, sometimes even a quarter. If she could gather together enough money she could tell Mama she'd made a deal and sold the cufflinks without the tie bar for three dollars. Adding up all the change she had a total of eighty-five cents. That meant she still needed two dollars and fifteen cents. How could she get two dollars and fifteen cents before going home? Retying her worn black and white saddle oxfords, an idea came to her. She didn't like it, but it was her only hope.

There was a man downtown that owned a car dealership. His name was Mr. McGinnis. Cheryl didn't like him at all, but she knew he had a lot of money. Mama took Cheryl there almost every Saturday. Parked in the alley behind the car dealership, she would slip Cheryl in the back door. Mr. McGinnis would be waiting by the door. He would hand Mama some money and she would leave. Cheryl knew Mama would go next door to the drugstore and buy some nerve medicine and some "Sen-Sen."

Mama almost always had "Sen-Sen" (tiny black licorice candies) in her mouth. Cheryl hated the smell of them. Then Mama would return to the car and sit with the other kids waiting for Mr.

McGinnis to thrust Cheryl out the back door and into the alley.

The first time Mama told her, "Cheryl, Mr. McGinnis is a nice man who is helping Mama. He likes you and wants to be your friend. You must be very nice to him and do whatever he asks you to. He has my permission, so don't you dare resist him. Do you understand? If you do, Mr. McGinnis will be very angry and he won't give me any money anymore. If that happens I will make you very, very sorry. Is that clear?"

It was very clear to Cheryl. She knew she dared not cross her mother, no matter what. Now, after several months of "visits" with Mr. McGinnis, Cheryl knew exactly what to expect. The steps that led to the basement of Mr. McGinnis' dealership were steep and dark. At the bottom of the stair was a light switch that Mr. McGinnis always clicked on. Cheryl believed there was no other light switch as loud as Mr. McGinnis'. Such a loud switch should have produced a lot of light, but it was connected to a lone red light bulb positioned directly above a long rectangular table.

On top of the table was a thick foam pad wrapped with a red-checkered oilcloth table covering. Mr. McGinnis would pick Cheryl up and lay her on the table with the light bulb positioned directly over her head.

It was always dim and damp in the basement and it smelled funny. Although she never saw the source, Cheryl would always hear water dripping. In the summertime she hated the oilcloth because it made her sweaty and sticky. It hurt when she was finally allowed to raise up because it pulled her skin.

Sometimes when Mr. McGinnis would undress her he would scowl at the bruises and sores on Cheryl. At first she thought he would help her by complaining to Mama about the bruising, but he just covered them over with ladies face powder.

Mr. McGinnis would take all kinds of pictures of Cheryl. Sometimes he would show some to her. He said he developed them himself right there in the basement. When he took pictures he would unscrew the red light bulb and replace it with a regular bulb. He had a silver umbrella that made the light seem bigger.

Sometimes a buzzer would sound and Mr. McGinnis would curse and command Cheryl to lie still without moving. The buzzer meant a customer had come in upstairs and he would have to tend to them. He warned her he'd be right back. He said there was a secret camera watching her and he could tell if she moved.

Cheryl would lie stiffly for what seemed long, extended periods of time, staring up at the bare light bulb suspended above her. She would pray for Jesus to forgive her. She knew He would because Mama and Mr. McGinnis were forcing her to do bad things. They always assured her there was nothing wrong with the pictures and the things Mr. McGinnis did, but their secrecy made Cheryl know they must be telling lies.

The Sunday school teacher taught the children to pray to God in Jesus' Name. Cheryl just couldn't do that. God was very scary to her and He was called "Heavenly Father." Fathers to Cheryl were very big, mean, strong, unloving and scary. Jesus was always described as gentle and loving and there were pictures of Him. You weren't supposed to paint or take a picture of God. He didn't want any pictures of Him. Cheryl loved Jesus and considered Him a very close and special friend. She didn't know what was holding Him back, but she was positive that someday He would come to her rescue.

She had told Jesus one dark, secret plan. Someday she was going to kill Mr. McGinnis. She hated him and the things that he did. Sometimes she hated Mama, too. She thought about killing Mama too, but the little kids still thought they needed Mama. The best solution was for Cheryl to die. The only difficulty with that solution was that she wouldn't be there to love and protect the little kids.

There was no obstacle like that with Mr. McGinnis. His children were all grown. He had a wife, though. Cheryl had seen her a couple of times from a distance. She looked mean. Cheryl wondered if Mr. McGinnis did hurting things to her, too. She'd probably be doing them both a favor by killing Mr. McGinnis.

I can't believe it, Cheryl thought. I'm going to Mr. McGinnis on my own. I really must be getting bad inside. I don't know if Jesus will forgive me. All the other times I've been forced to go. This time I'm going on my own. But, there's no other way to get the money that fast. Maybe Mr. McGinnis will just loan it to me. I could pay him back little by little out of my tips from people.

"Jesus, please forgive me before I go and after I go. You've got to understand. I have to get the money or Mama will beat me terrible for losing the cufflink. If You get really mad at me, just make me really sick or strike me dead. I won't even be mad and I won't complain, just so I'd get to come and live with You."

After being at Mr. McGinnis' garage, Cheryl always felt dirty and vulgar. Vulgar was Mama's word. She wasn't sure what that meant – but it was bad. It sounded mean and nasty and dirty. It felt like everyone looked at her accusingly, like they knew what she'd been doing. Low and deep inside her stomach she had terrible cramps, relentless pain, and aching that lasted for days. Sometimes her stomach would swell and she could not go to the bathroom. Mama would make her drink bunches of water, forcing her to drink so much at once she felt she would smother or drown. It helped to sleep on her side, her knees drawn up with a pillow or blanket stuffed between her knees and chest.

Cheryl was in the alley now by Mr. McGinnis' back door. No, she thought, I'm not going to go sneaking in the back door. I'm going in the front. She walked around to the front of the building and slipped in the front door. Weaving past the shiny new cars she made her way to the office.

Mr. McGinnis stood up when he saw her approaching. "What are you doing here?" He looked mad.

Cheryl suppressed the desire to talk back or to run out of the building. As quickly as possible she explained her dilemma to Mr. McGinnis.

"Two dollars and fifteen cents, huh? That's a lot of money." He squatted down on his knees so he was eye to eye with her. "Let's see what we can work out." As he reached down and pushed the plastic dry cleaner bag up to her waist, Cheryl closed her eyes. She didn't think Jesus would listen to her praying in this situation, but it was worth a try. Maybe at least He would let "The Black" come swallow her up before Mr. McGinnis hurt her.

The sharp clicking of high heels jolted Cheryl and Mr. McGinnis. He dropped the plastic bag and shot straight up. Dropping back down he hissed at Cheryl. "It's my wife! Get out one of your boxes and act like you're selling it to me. Hurry up!"

Cheryl quickly pulled out the box with the missing cufflink. In a voice that was nervously too loud he said, "Okay, little girl, how much for the set?"

"Five dollars with the tie bar, sir." Cheryl considered confronting Mr. McGinnis with his wife standing right there. No, there'd be Mama to face if that happened. Besides, Mama had told her over and over again that the police and judges and courts never believe children. She said they only believe adults and put lying children in dungeons with rats and snakes until they admit they lied. Mr. McGinnis stuffed a five-dollar bill in her hand and snatched the box away from her.

"There's your money. Now go home."

"Thank you, Mr. McGinnis," Cheryl said. She pushed past him and brushed by Mrs. McGinnis without looking up or making eye contact. She felt very guilty around Mrs. McGinnis, but she was never happier to see anyone as she was to see Mrs. McGinnis walk in. Maybe Jesus had heard her after all. She'd sold the cufflink set, had the five dollars to give to Mama, and she could still keep the eighty-five cents for herself. The best part was Mr. McGinnis hadn't touched her with her permission.

It was a wonderful feeling of control. Jesus might still be upset that she had considered going on her own to see Mr. McGinnis, but not as mad as He might have been had she been forced to go through with it. Cheryl felt pretty confident Mr. McGinnis wouldn't tell Mama. He wouldn't risk making her angry with him. It was dark now and beginning to snow. Cheryl ran toward home. Throwing open the front door she was blasted with suffocating heat. She quickly adjusted though and shook the jewelry boxes from her sweater. The radiator hissed as she laid the soggy sweater across it. A chill spread over her as she peeled off the plastic sack. Mama appeared from the bedroom with her purse under her arm. "Where's the money from what you sold?" she demanded.

Cheryl cheerfully handed over the five-dollar bill. "I sold the tiger-eye set," she said.

"Well, don't get too comfortable. I need you to run to the store for me. There's a blizzard coming and we need some things. Here's a list - and hurry. It's already dark. Why did you stay out so late anyway?" Mama eyed her suspiciously.

"I wasn't having any luck and I knew we needed the money, so I just kept on until I finally sold the tiger-eye set." Cheryl justified this little deception. It sort of was the truth. Just to be on the safe side with Jesus, she'd crossed her fingers behind her back when she'd answered Mama.

The snow was already swirling down around as she walked briskly to the grocery store. She dashed through the door just before the owner locked it. "I just have to get a few things for my mama," she called breathlessly back over her shoulder.

Running down the familiar aisles she quickly gathered the items on the list: a loaf of bread, a box of instant milk, a carton of half and half for Mama, coffee, four cans of chicken noodle soup, tomato soup (Mama knew Cheryl hated tomato soup) and melba toast. Cheryl dumped everything on the counter for the man to ring up. He managed to get it into one sack.

"Are you sure you can carry this? It's almost as big as you," the store man questioned.

"Oh sure, I'm used to carrying lots of weight." Cheryl assured him.

"Well, you'd better hurry home. This blizzard is already bad." The force of the wind and the driving, swirling snow took her breath away as she pushed her way down Main Street toward home. It was impossible to see the other side of the street for all the snow piled down the center. Cheryl crossed at the end of the fifth block. Now she had to do some weaving through residential streets. The plastic rain bonnet had been blown down around her neck and was crackling in the wind.

The snow was more intense, seeming to drive tiny needles into her eyes. She tilted her face toward the sack and lowered her head to avoid being pelted by the snow and sleet. Her face felt numb from the cold and her ears were burning. She could feel herself loosening her grip on the sack as her bare fingers succumbed to the relentless bitter cold.

The saddle oxfords leaked and her wet socks seemed to magnify the intensity of the icy cold. Her feet felt heavy as she struggled to continue, pressing against the powerful wind. Soon she realized with despair that she was hopelessly lost. Dropping the burdensome bag of groceries, she huddled against a light pole and began to cry. The zipper on her jacket was broken and she couldn't keep it pulled together with her stiff, unyielding fingers. In quiet surrender to the elements she knelt in the snow, with her head bent down and waited to die.

It was no use to ask Jesus to help. She could tell she'd made Him very sad by going to see Mr. McGinnis. This was her punishment. It was okay really, because she would get to go to heaven to live with Jesus. She wished she'd have known ahead of time. It would have given her a chance to say goodbye to Davey, Eddie, Richie, Kati, and Kari. She would have told them that she was going to heaven to get her wings and become a guardian angel for them. Cheryl felt warmth creeping through her body. It made her very peaceful and sleepy. Huddling next to the light pole and hugging the grocery bag, she closed her eyes.

The sensation of being lifted awakened Cheryl. She turned and slowly opened her eyes expecting to see an angel. Startled, she came face to face with a man with a furry black hat and wearing steamed-over black-rimmed glasses. The snow and sleet pelted her face and forced her to close her eyes again. The man lifted her into a warm car and put the groceries in at her feet. Pulling a blanket from the back seat, he wrapped her in it and got in and slammed his door shut. He seemed very angry and was muttering under his breath.

He turned to Cheryl. "I know who you are. You're Hank Morgan's granddaughter, aren't you?" Cheryl nodded, a little less frightened at the mention of Grandpa Morgan's name. She shook her head to clear her groggy mind.

"Well, Hank and Anna are sure going to hear about this. It's a blizzard and here you are out here without a scarf or hat or mittens. You don't have on snow pants or boots. You don't even have knee socks or tights on your legs. Look at your jacket. The zipper's broken. What kind of mother would send you out in this weather, and dressed like that?"

Frightened by his ranting and raving, Cheryl grew more troubled at the mention of her mother. "It's okay, Mister," she insisted. "I'm okay now. You can just drop me off." The man had somehow found her house and had pulled up in front. The snow was still swirling and getting heavier. She watched it spin and dance in the glow of his headlights.

"I know this is where you live. I'm going to give your mother a piece of my mind. Why, if I hadn't come along you would have frozen to death in that snowdrift. Look! Your face, ears and hands are fiery red. I'll bet you've got some frostbite to say the least. You're just lucky I had some business in this little town or I wouldn't have been here to find you. They would have dug you out next spring."

The man lifted Cheryl out of the car, still wrapped in the blanket and grabbed the sack of groceries. With a few rapid, purposeful steps he was pounding noisily on Bea's front door.

Davey, opening the door, stood looking astonished to see Cheryl riding high in the arms of a tall stranger. "Mama," he called, "There's a big man here, and he's got Cheryl."

Bea approached the door and scrutinized the man standing in the doorway. He broke the silence. In an angry, loud tone he said, "Lady, I'm the lawyer that defended your husband. Hank and Anna Morgan are good friends of mine and believe you me; they're going to hear about this!" He set Cheryl down.

"Your little girl was lost in the blizzard. I found her collapsed in a snowdrift almost unconscious. If I hadn't come along she'd be dead by now. Look at how she's dressed. What kind of a mother are you?"

The man was very mad. He was shouting and pointing his finger and shaking it at Mama as he talked. The children all gathered in a tight cluster in the corner beside the door. They were afraid the man was going to take them away from Mama and from each other. Cheryl could tell Mama was getting mad, too.

Mama finally blew up. She yelled and cussed at the man and told him to mind his own business. With a sudden thrust she forced him out the doorway and slammed the door shut.

"You haven't heard the last of me, lady!" The man was bellowing through the securely fastened door. The children heard his boots crunching across the snow as he stomped back to his car. The car door slammed. He raced his engine, and with screeching tires, roared off into the night.

Mama started laughing. The children were skeptical about joining in. They stayed in their tight circle by the door. "That man's a real nut!" Mama picked up the groceries and headed for the kitchen. She turned, expecting the children were following her. Observing them still standing frozen in the living room, she beckoned them toward the kitchen. "Let's celebrate and make some cookies." Cheryl nudged them. "Get in there quick before she changes her mind." Cheryl didn't know what they could be celebrating, but while Mama was distracted it was best to just play along with her.

Mama and Cheryl mixed up the dough for peanut butter cookies and formed them into balls. The other children stood poised with forks, ready to mark them for the oven. It was a warm circle inside as the wind and snow whirled outside. Mama made another special treat, vanilla milk. She had Cheryl mix the powdered milk with water in a saucepan. Adding vanilla and sugar, it was heated until warm and poured into coffee cups. Davey especially liked the vanilla milk.

One time Cheryl had climbed up into the cabinet and gotten down the vanilla. She called Davey over and loaded a tablespoon with the pure, sweet smelling vanilla flavoring. She knew from experience that vanilla was a deceptive liquid. This didn't deter her from letting Davey discover that for himself. Trusting her, Davey eagerly swallowed the entire spoonful only to involuntarily spew the bitter liquid all over the kitchen. Cheryl knew it had been mean, but nonetheless she laughed until her sides hurt as Davey rinsed and rinsed to rid his taste buds of the prohibited nip of vanilla.

By age twelve he began running away from home. In front of authorities Davey's dad Renny would appear to be the perfect father, giving intense lectures on the consequences of illegal behavior. At home where the only witnesses had taken a vow of silence, Davey was mercilessly beaten and whipped. Verbal assaults with an onslaught of derogatory remarks roared at him and, punctuated with hard kicks to the stomach and rib cage and fists to his face, arms and stomach, created invisible wounds that scarred his life forever.

Renny also seemed to relish displaying his brute strength by grabbing the boys up by the neck and holding them a foot or two off the floor. He would lift them by the neck to his eye level and accent his words by pounding their heads against the wall. With their faces purple, eyes bulging and pounding, heads aching and windpipes causing pain and fear, Renny would abruptly tire of the "game" and drop Davey or Eddie or Richie to the floor. He'd walk away, leaving them in a small, injured, and crumpled heap on the floor.

All three boys grew very bitter and resentful at early ages and eventually became hardened to abuse. Individually, and unknown to the other two, each plotted the murder of Renny. Davey plotted a quick, simple murder of his abuser with a single shotgun blast or a quick snap of the neck.

Eddie wanted his father/tormentor to suffer. He devised plans that involved poison, fire, axes or anything that would cause severe pain and a slow, violent death.

Richie contrived different ways he could get hold of a butcher knife and plunge it through the heart of Renny. The plan had a serious flaw though. Richie doubted that Renny actually had a heart. For the moment, though, the children were full from the peanut butter cookies and warm and sleepy from the hot vanilla milk. Bea and Cheryl settled all five into bed for the night. Bea motioned for Cheryl to come sit in her bedroom doorway. As she prepared for bed, Bea instructed Cheryl about the lawyer.

"Cheryl, if the welfare people come and question you, you must say that you had on a warm coat and mittens and snow pants and boots. You'll have to say the lawyer is lying. Tell them that you had just slipped and fallen in the snow and that he scared you by just grabbing you up and forcing you to get into the car with him." Cheryl listened passively, submissive to her mother's instruction. "Do you have it clear in your mind what to say? You'll have to be solid. You can't change your story once you tell it. Let's practice." Bea looked tense. Confirming Cheryl's suspicions, Bea reached for her "nerve medicine" and popped a few tablets. After a few minutes of rehearsal, Bea appeared satisfied that Cheryl could discredit the lawyer's incident report and sent her off to bed.

As Cheryl lay in bed, she wondered why Mama would have her lie to the welfare lady about the lawyer. She knew Mama was afraid there might be trouble, but Mama had always said that the courts and police and everyone never believe children over adults. That could pose a real problem for Mama if that lawyer did go to the authorities.

Oh well, it wasn't her problem right now. Mama would have to worry about that later. Probably the lawyer wouldn't do anything anyway. Other attempts to intervene on behalf of the Morgan children had always vaporized. Cheryl wasn't going to waste her time thinking about it anymore. It was hard to have hope for change only to have that hope crushed when people didn't do what they said. Cheryl had to remind herself that it was futile to believe that someone would actually do something to help them. She tucked the blanket around her sisters and closed her eyes. The warmth of their bodies pressed against hers was comforting as she lay listening to the howling wind outside. Thankfully she was inside and warm and dry. That was good enough for now.

TEN

Like dew drops on a rosebud, tiny beads of sweat in Kari's platinum curls glistened in the late summer sun. The heat made Kati's heavy glasses slide down her nose so often she tired of pushing them back up. Instead she would throw her head back and look down her nose through the wayward lenses. The boys were lolling in the cool grass in the shade of an old mulberry tree. Bea had forbidden the children to eat the mulberries, but they ate them anyway.

The old lady next door had shown them the secret of using a stalk of rhubarb to remove the telltale mulberry stains from their teeth and skin. The boys had eaten their fill of the fat, juicy berries and erased the evidence with the rhubarb. Now they were lazily watching Cheryl and Kati create lei necklaces using string and hollyhock blooms. Kari toddled back and forth between her sisters and the hollyhocks, carefully bearing one bloom at a time.

Cheryl had celebrated her ninth birthday that summer. Davey was eight, Eddie seven, Richie six, Kati five, and Kari was three and a half. Kari was the measure of Renny's imprisonment. In conversations overheard Cheryl concluded that his long-awaited homecoming was about to take place. All the children were anxious for him to return home. Though the memories of Renny were dim and splintered, the children all agreed that life would surely be easier and better once they had a daddy again.

Children can be vultures toward the wounded in their midst. The Morgan children had often been the targeted morsels, picked apart, ripped up and ridiculed by their peers. The mysterious, ever elusive "they" in playground hierarchies always found out that the Morgans were poor; their daddy was a "jailbird", their mother "white trash". "They" also discovered that the children were unusually resilient, hardy victims of their taunting insults. Cheryl and Davey would collect Eddie and Richie from their classes, and united, they could make the journey home at least physically unhindered.

Even in church the younger children refused to be separated from the older children. The teachers tolerated the behavior. Cheryl and Davey imagined themselves the parents and rather enjoyed the sense of responsibility and importance. Cheryl always kept Kari close to her, Davey watched over Kati, and Eddie always had a little shadow named Richie. The three sets of children thus teamed would "adopt" a couple in the church to sit with on Sunday. In the calm atmosphere of the service the children would often nap nestled against each other and their much-admired adult friends.

Though it appeared impolite to sleep and doze through service, it provided a brief escape from harsh reality for the Morgan children. They could rest and slumber in the pews without fear of being ripped and jerked out of sleep to violence. They were touched by hands that didn't seek to hurt them. Often they were fed little treats they didn't otherwise get -- candy, gum, popcorn, cookies and fruit.

Church was the one place they felt safe and secure. Even though they sensed many times they were not as readily accepted as the clean, well-dressed children, they were willing to accept any shred of compassion and charity bestowed on them.

Church was a sanctuary, a tangible refuge from the turbulent daily lifestyle the children were accustomed to. Most of all, they got to experience and to see visible glimpses of hope, of peaceful lives, of loving families, of people to look up to and to say, "Someday I'm gonna be just like him, or just like her."

It has to be understood that in the Morgan children's abusive situation sometimes the only things that held each child were faith in God (in Jesus), and hope that someday they'd grow up and get away from it. Also, there was love for each other, and an overpowering motivation to protect against separation from each other at all costs.

That was the incentive for them not to tell, or to lie when questioned. They'd withhold truth and maintain protection of Renny and Bea by saying, "I fell down," "I tripped," "I got in a fight," or "We had a wreck." The other alternative was to simply stay at home, hidden away until the bruising and swelling went down. It meant as they grew older that they took zeros in gym because they refused to dress out or shower in class.

They were always threatened that if they told they would be

separated into an orphanage or foster homes and would never see each other again. Once when Cheryl, Davey and Richie were all badly swollen and bruised from a beating, Cheryl crept out of the house as Bea lay sleeping one afternoon. With a little brother on each hand, she walked deliberately the few blocks to a police station.

Standing across the street, a beaten, bruised, bloody little brother on each hand, she stood debating if the police would really hurt or help them. Heart pounding and praying for courage, Cheryl sadly turned, and defeated, took the boys back home. She couldn't bring herself to take the chance.

Bea leaned out the back screen door now and bellowed for the children to come inside. Immediately they all jumped up and ran to the house. The littler ones didn't bother opening the door. The screen was torn out on two sides enabling them to enter through the screen. Gathering on the floor in front of the fan aimed at Bea's big chair, they waited for her to speak.

Bea's face was flushed and they could tell she was excited. She gave the announcement Cheryl was expecting. "Daddy is coming home on Saturday, isn't that wonderful?! Grandpa Morgan is going to bring him this weekend. We're going to move and get a real house and have a daddy again."

The three youngest children were immediately affected by the excitement in Bea's voice. They jumped up and down and hugged each other and celebrated in their innocent childish enthusiasm. Cheryl and Davey, though excited, were more cautious, and Eddie too was leery. Vague, oppressive, negative recollections of life with Daddy disturbed the fantasy they so wanted to believe. It would be refreshing to have a home of their own, food to eat whenever they were hungry, and most of all, a daddy who wasn't a "jailbird."

The rest of the week was spent rearranging furniture, packing boxes, and making cookies and fudge for Renny's arrival. The children ran to the front porch anytime they heard a vehicle approaching. Finally it was Grandpa Morgan's De Soto coming toward them. All six children and Bea came pouring out of the house to meet them. Grandpa and Daddy were waving out the windows, and the car bounced as he pulled in the driveway. Bea ran to Renny and he hugged and kissed her, picking her up and spinning her around.

The children had converged on Grandpa Morgan. Now he had Kati and Kari in his arms, a child hanging from every appendage. His burdened legs dragging, he lugged them over to Renny. One by one the children let loose of their grandpa and dropped to the ground. Kari alone stayed attached to Grandpa Morgan. Renny reached for her. "So, this is little Kari, huh? Come see Daddy." Kari buried her face in Grandpa Morgan's neck. Renny gently tugged at her. Kari began screaming and clutched fiercely to her grandfather.

Bea shook her head and slipped her hand in Renny's. "Let her adjust a little. She's not use to men. Come see the other children and how they've grown."

Cheryl stepped forward first. "Look how big I am, Daddy. I'm going to start the fourth grade in the fall."

"You are a big girl, Cheryl." Renny reached in his pocket and pulled out a dollar bill. "I didn't know what to get for a big girl like you, so I brought you a whole dollar for yourself. You can buy whatever you want."

Renny turned to Bea. "She has grown. It's too bad about her teeth though. Where'd she get such big front teeth? She'd be pretty if her teeth weren't so big and crooked."

Bea nodded her agreement. "I tell her if she has to smile it needs to be with her lips together, mouth closed. She usually doesn't forget herself like that. It's just the excitement of your coming home." Bea scowled at Cheryl. "Get back. Let your brothers greet your dad."

Cheryl's countenance had darkened, but Renny and Bea were oblivious to the change. She wanted to give him a chance, but she didn't think she was going to like Renny being back home, except for the money part. She could tell that now she was going to be ousted from her position as confidant to her mother. It was also very offensive that Renny talked about her as if she wasn't present. She'd be sure to keep her mouth closed around him. She didn't want to display her unattractive teeth in his presence again anytime soon.

Mama lined up the boys according to age. She'd shaved their heads for the occasion, and their white scalps shined in contrast to their freckled, suntanned faces. Renny noted that Eddie, though younger than Davey, was taller, and that Richie was still very small for his age. Reaching into his duffle bag he pulled out three squirt guns and handed one to each of the boys. "I've already filled them with water. You boys can go have a squirt gun battle. Go on now, go play."

Reluctantly, the little boys edged away from Renny. When they felt they'd retreated a safe distance they excitedly began examining the guns. Soon they discovered how they worked and began shooting each other.

Renny had a shiny, bright red, spongy ball for Kati and a little stuffed animal for Kari. Kati withdrew with her ball and stood back over with Grandpa Morgan and Cheryl. Kari accepted the stuffed animal but kept her face buried in Grandpa's neck.

"Daddy, Daddy, our guns are empty. How do we make them squirt again?" Davey ran up to Renny with Eddie and Richie close at his heels. Renny looked at them incredulously. "How did you ever raise such stupid boys?" He glared at Bea. "They can't even figure out how to refill a squirt gun."

The boys stepped back as he reached toward them. "Well, you boys are just too stupid to have squirt guns. You little morons. Here's what happens to little morons' guns." Renny snatched the guns out of the little boys' hands. Hurling them to the ground in disgust, he descended on them with his gigantic foot and crushed all three in a single blow. "That takes care of that problem now, doesn't it, boys?" Renny was laughing and shaking his head. Bea laughed too. Arm in arm Bea and Renny disappeared into the house. Cheryl heard Renny mutter, "Little idiots."

Grandpa Morgan looked ashamed. He expected the little boys to cry, but they just silently came and stood next to him. Hank had to brush it off; it was out of his hands. Gathering the children around him, he passed out cookies from Grandma. From under the car seat he pulled the anticipated jar full of pennies.

The boys were old enough now to help with dividing, so Cheryl sat on the ground with Kati and Kari, rolling the new red ball back and forth. Gazing toward the house, she tried to envision what life would be like with Renny back home. It sure seemed to her that he was still kind of mean. Surely, though, Mama would be much happier. That could only work for the good of everyone concerned. Cheryl was skeptical but allowed herself to be hopeful. A new home of their own and having a daddy again did sound wonderful.

* * *

Grandpa and Grandma Morgan kept their word and bought a home for Renny and his family. Grandpa Morgan was a welder and a coal miner and farmer. He had always been very frugal. His conservative manner was reflected in the home he purchased for Renny. It was a small, two-bedroom frame home. There was a screened-in porch on the back and a full porch across the front. The yard was narrow but deep. Back toward the alley stood an outhouse and a lean-to storage shed open across the front. The children immediately claimed this as their playhouse. They were elated at the luxury of such a non-essential. Amazingly enough, Renny and Bea demonstrated no reluctance in allowing them to have it as a playhouse.

Renny quickly found a job working on a construction crew. He was on "parole," Bea told the children. "Parole," she explained, "is a proving time that you are required to report to the police everything good that you do. You must show them that you will not disobey the law ever again."

"Or at least not get caught at it," Renny added, winking at Bea.

Renny would get scraps of lumber and building materials from his job and haul them home in the back of the station wagon.

Evenings would be spent working on the house. On the weekends Grandpa Morgan would come down and help. The first project was to turn the screened-in back porch into a bedroom for the girls. The floor sloped downward, but Renny said that wouldn't be a problem for the girls. With the porch closed in, a double bed and a chest of drawers were positioned close to the door leading from the kitchen. Grandpa said that would help in the winter so they'd be closer to the radiator located in the living room.

One weekend soon after they moved into the little house Grandpa Morgan brought a very special surprise for the children. "Now that you have your own house and a yard," he said, "there's something else that's absolutely necessary to have." With that he'd pulled a little taffy-colored puppy from behind his back. It had little white feet and the tip of her tail was black. Being the oldest, Cheryl got to name her. "Tippy" became the newest member of the Morgan household, and the children loved her from the instant they saw her.

Bea was very indignant about the fact she had to traipse out to the outhouse to use the facilities, especially in the night. There was a pump by the kitchen sink. Renny said he could run water from the pump and install a toilet inside. The boys' small bedroom backed up to the kitchen. Using plywood and paneling he divided the boys' room in half. Several days and drawings later he had devised a plan that he knew would work. He built a bunk bed three beds high.

Attaching it to the wall and making each bunk wide enough for the mattress, he could fit a row of shelves on the opposite wall for their clothes and belongings. The boys loved it. Davey especially enjoyed his bunk at the very top. He had to remember, though, not to sit up in bed or he would bump his head on the ceiling. It was kind of hot in the summer, but he had the warmest spot in the winter.

The other half of the bedroom was converted into an indoor bathroom for Renny and Bea. He installed a commode and a sink and hooked up the wringer washer. The children were still required to use the outhouse. Bea said they were too messy and didn't appreciate nice things.

Grandma Morgan found a big black cast iron kettle with a handle like a bucket on it. She also bought a big washtub. On Saturday nights Cheryl and Davey would heat water in the kettle and fill the washtub. It would be set out in the girls' bedroom because their floor slanted downward and the water would run out along the floorboards. One by one the children would bathe according to age, the youngest to the oldest, adding more hot water every other child.

Bea complained of the summer heat, so Renny promised he would build her an air conditioner. The children knew no one who had air conditioning in their home. "We must be getting rich," Cheryl and Davey decided. Fashioning a box out of wood scraps, Renny attached it outside in the window next to Bea's chair. He took a hand drill and made neat rows of tiny holes in the bottom of the box. Next he laid straw mats inside. Going into the house he took a fan and set it up inside the box facing backwards. He had frozen some blocks of ice and placed them in the box so the fan blew across them.

Kari did the honors of plugging in the fan. They all stood

back and felt the delicious cool air magically flow past them. It worked! Daddy must be one of the smartest men in the world! He might be mean sometimes, but life was getting to be a little easier now that he was back home.

The week before school started, Renny had finished the renovations on the house. Hank and Anna came to visit and celebrate with them. Renny was especially proud of the linoleum he installed in the kitchen and the newly created bathroom and floor furnace in the living room. He had gotten the linoleum and an old floor furnace at an auction for ten dollars and installed them both without Hank's help.

The children were sorry that their grandparents lived so far away now. Bea had confided in Cheryl that the prison psychologist had told them that for Renny, the farther away he was from his mother, the better off he'd be. Cheryl didn't understand that. She loved Grandma Morgan and couldn't see how being far away from her would make Daddy a better person. She knew Mama didn't like Grandma though, and she had detected that the feeling was mutual. Also, she had to consider that doctors were very intelligent. A person would be ignorant not to follow a doctor's instructions.

Hank and Anna brought with them the traditional beginning of school gifts for the children, new socks and underwear for all. For each of the school age children they brought two red "Big Chief" tablets, two #2 pencils, and a box of crayons. The littler ones, abandoned at home with the start of school, each got a consolation package of a box of crayons and a coloring book. They were getting ready to leave when Grandma Morgan pulled Cheryl aside.

"Cheryl, you're getting to be a big girl now. You need to try to help your mother more, keeping the house and children clean. This place is filthier than a pigsty. I don't know how you stand this mess."

"Grandma, I try, but those mean old boys always mess everything up again. I'm a good cook though. I do almost all the cooking for Mama." Cheryl saw Mama eyeing her suspiciously. It made her nervous. She knew she'd get in trouble for talking to Grandma alone. Mama would accuse her and Grandma of "conspiring" together against her.

Cheryl wasn't sure what "conspiring" was, but she knew Mama was strongly opposed to it. She decided it wasn't worth it to try to defend herself to Grandma. "Okay, Grandma, I'll try real hard to keep everything nicer." She didn't want to hurt Grandma's feelings, but Mama had had her working on the house all week getting everything cleaned up for their visit. It looked much better than usual. "I have to go now." With that Cheryl ran over and stood close to her mother.

Grandpa Morgan was honking the horn as Grandma hurried down the front steps. Renny and Bea and all the children lined across the porch, waving goodbye until they drove out of sight.

"Well, I think for once we passed inspection," Renny was standing behind Bea, gently rubbing her neck and shoulders.

"How about it, Cheryl?" Bea glared at her. "Did we pass inspection under Grandma's evil eye?"

Cheryl purposed to gaze directly but not too directly into Mama's eyes as she answered. "Yes, Mama, I believe we did."

"See there, what'd I tell you?" Renny was satisfied. Bea kept her gaze fixed on Cheryl. Cheryl felt it but restrained herself from squirming.

"Come on, let's head for bed." Renny turned Bea toward the door. "Cheryl, you get these little rascals to bed. We'll see everybody in the morning. Make sure you turn out all the lights. Davey, that's your job."

Cheryl knew it was still early. The lightning bugs were just coming out. She dare not argue though, so dutifully the children all headed for bed. It was hot and stuffy on the back porch even with the windows open. Mosquitoes were buzzing in the dark. She could hear the moths hitting the back porch light that illumined nocturnal visits to the outhouse. Enough time had passed that it would soon be time to turn the pillow to the cool side, and then perhaps she could fall asleep.

The past few weeks with Daddy back home had been relatively peaceful. He had exploded a few times, as had Mama, but it was all mild in comparison to the violence the children had become accustomed to. A bad thing had happened several times, though. Daddy had exposed himself to the girls. One time while Bea was at the beauty shop Cheryl had walked in on him and was shocked at what she saw.

Daddy was lying naked on the bed. Beside him were Kari, Kati, and one of Kati's neighborhood friends. They had a sheet, which Renny had folded down to resemble a diaper. Daddy was raising his hips up as the little girls struggled to get the "diaper" under him. Cheryl stood paralyzed in the doorway watching as they finally got the giant diaper fastened on him.

Suddenly Daddy had noticed Cheryl standing in the door-way. He gave each of the little girls some candy and a quarter and told them he had to quit "playing house" and get back to work. Cheryl stayed as if glued to the doorframe. Once the little girls were outside, Renny advanced threateningly toward Cheryl. His diaper dropped to the floor.

"Go get Tippy and bring her to me, Cheryl." He stepped out of the diaper. "You'd better be back in here by the time I get dressed." Her heart pulsating out of her chest, Cheryl went calling for Tippy. She hoped Tippy wouldn't come but was afraid of what would happen to her if she were unable to produce Tippy.

Where were the boys? She could hear them outside. They were probably at their friend's house across the alley. She wished Kati and Kari would come back inside. Not a chance though. She could see them out front sitting on the curb eating and playing with their Lifesaver candies. She called Tippy's name one more time. Renny was opening the bedroom door. Just as she heard him step up behind her, Tippy came slowly out from under the sofa, yawning and stretching from one of her many naps. Cheryl scooped her up and held her close. Renny was looking out the front window at the little girls. "Where are the boys?" he demanded.

"I don't know, I think they're across the alley. Daddy, what are you going to do? Tippy didn't do anything bad. I won't tell about your game with the little girls." Cheryl wished Mama would hurry up and get back from the beauty shop.

Renny had a belt in his hand, folded in half. He was making it snap as he stood over her. "Let's go to the shed out back. Bring

146

Tippy."

Cheryl turned the pillow over to the cool side, remembering. She didn't like to think about what had happened next. Renny had taken Tippy and fastened the belt around her middle. Then, taking it like a whip, drawn it back again and again, beating poor little Tippy against the side of the shed until she was dead. He had forced Cheryl to pick up the limp, bloody puppy and wrap it in newspaper and put it in the trashcan back by the alley. "If you ever tell anyone, Cheryl, this is what will happen to you," he'd warned. With that, he turned and strolled calmly back into the house.

That night Cheryl had slipped out of bed and gotten Tippy out of the trashcan. She couldn't stand the thought of the little puppy being burned in the trashcan. Slipping across the alley to the neighbors, she borrowed a spade. By the light of the moon, softened by her tear-brimmed eyes, she'd dug a grave for Tippy. With the ground stomped back down she pulled some grass and gathered gravel to scatter across the top to camouflage the new grave. Cheryl buried Tippy in the ground, but that day she also buried anger, bitterness and murderous hatred in her heart that festered there for years.

She had never been to a funeral, but she said some words over Tippy she felt fitting. Heavy with sorrow, she slipped back into bed and sought comfort from her invisible confidant, Jesus. That night was the first time she saw a falling star. She took it as an omen that Jesus/God was listening to the lonely, sad little girl. It gave her hope that perhaps she was not so isolated from love as her circumstances made her feel.

It was time to turn the pillow again. Cheryl shifted Kati and

Kari to new places on the mattress to help them get cooler too. Both of their heads and faces were sweaty. Although she longed for someone to confide in about Tippy, she was glad her brothers and sisters had been spared the truth. They still believed Tippy had run away and would someday return. Grass was now growing over the little mound of dirt next to the clothesline post. "Someday, I'm going to tell them it was Daddy that killed Tippy." With that, Cheryl turned over again and went to sleep.

ELEVEN

B ea was shrieking as she ran switching on lights and shaking children awake. "Get up, get up!" It was picture day at school and Cheryl wanted to look perfect.

Cheryl's teacher, Mrs. Bates, had said she liked profile pictures of girls with ponytails. Taking note that Cheryl was smiling wide at the mention of ponytails, Mrs. Bates clarified herself by adding, "Not a dragged-down ponytail in the middle of the back of your head like Cheryl Morgan, but a high, full, swinging ponytail like Robbin." Robbin tossed her head, causing her ponytail to swing in a pendulum motion. With her nose high in the air, Robbin stuck out her tongue at Cheryl.

Cheryl wasn't very well liked at school. She was dirty and poorly dressed. She ate lunch on the free lunch program, and the other children said she smelled funny. Cheryl was very bold and bossy and often got into fights.

Although her teachers would always acknowledge how intel-

ligent Cheryl was and how well she tested, because of her responsibilities at home, she was rarely able to turn in homework or major
projects. She was never equipped for school and missed classes
quite often. Usually she was late and almost never wore clean or
matched clothing. Her long brown hair hung in separated dirty
strands that she sometimes pulled up into a crooked ponytail.
None of the Morgan children brushed their teeth and typically
had dirt-streaked hands and faces. Their feet, when stripped of
dirty, holey, unmatched socks, were encrusted with dirt and grime.
They suffered from frequent bouts with impetigo, ringworm and
lice.

Despite these challenges, they all were excited about picture
day. Grandma Morgan had sent a check to the school and this
year they were actually going to get to keep their school pictures.
Cheryl helped the younger children finish getting ready then carried a brush and a rubber band to Mama.

"Mama, will you please make me a high ponytail for pictures?" Cheryl asked, handing her the hairbrush. Mama pulled,
brushed, and yanked impatiently at the snarls in Cheryl's hair.
Cheryl tried to stand still, but it was hurting her head and making
her eyes water. Finally she cried out a long "Ow-w-w-w-w!"

"That does it!" Mama threw the hairbrush across the room
and flew into her bedroom, muttering angrily. She reappeared
with a pair of scissors. Before Cheryl could react, Bea reached out
and gathered all her hair in one hand. With one stroke she clipped
off Cheryl's hair to just below her ears.

"Now," said Bea smugly as she waved the foot-long lock of
hair, "we won't have any whining about snarls anymore, will we?"

Cheryl ran crying out to the outhouse and latched the door. With her fists she beat the walls and door of the tiny structure until she was exhausted. Finally, heeding the pleas of her younger brothers and sisters, she came out. The boys tried to comfort her, their own newly "crew-cut" shaven heads shining, "It looks nice, Cheryl, and you look real pretty."

The boys had attached an old rear-view mirror to the side of the outhouse. Inspecting Bea's impulsive butchering through red, swollen eyes, Cheryl again burst into tears.

Bea came walking across the yard. "Oh, quit your crying. It looks fine. You needed it cut anyway." Bea was still holding the ponytail. "Now, get to school before you get in trouble for being late." She patted Cheryl on the shoulder. "It'll make a nice picture. Here, let me comb your bangs down and straighten out your part." Cheryl obediently stood still while Mama worked with her hair. "Come in the house. I'll put a little hair spray on it." This was unbelievable. Mama never let anyone use her hair spray. The new haircut held down with a misting of hair spray, Cheryl and the kids filed out the back door and down the alley toward school. It was slightly comforting to Cheryl that Mama appeared somewhat remorseful over the impromptu haircut.

* * *

Mama loved long hair and had always made the girls keep their hair long. She said it was pleasing to God. They could never braid their hair, though, because that was a sin. Mama said it was written right in the Bible. Even though Mama didn't often go to church, she always sent the children. From the time Cheryl could remember, Mama let it be known that she didn't believe in divorce, smoking, drinking or dancing. Mama had learned about God while attending her Aunt Frances' church and at missions school with Renny.

Aunt Frances was rich, and if anything was good enough for Aunt Frances, it was good enough for Mama. Aunt Frances wouldn't speak to Mama since she'd married Renny. Nonetheless, Mama wrote to her faithfully.

Cheryl knew from their late night conversations (before Daddy had returned home) that Mama did in her own way regret "flying off the handle." She did firmly believe, though, that a child didn't learn a lesson unless blood was drawn. She knew you weren't supposed to cuss in church, and she wished she didn't cuss at all.

One thing Mama was afraid of was burning in hell. Sometimes Mama would make all the children go without food and water for a day or two. She would let them feel how dreadful it was to be hungry and especially thirsty. Mama would tell about the Bible story of how the rich man would feed the poor man scraps from his table. Then, when the rich man died and went to hell, he begged for the poor man to dip his fingertip into water and just wet his tongue.

Mama said that was hell, never a drop of water for a person's dry, swollen tongue. The list of things that sent a person to hell got longer the older the children got. Cheryl sometimes wondered if they were practicing for hell. It didn't seem that bad, until Mama said hell never ends – it goes on and on and on and on for all eternity. Thinking about that too much made Cheryl feel very dark and hopeless. She thought real hell would be having no hope that your suffering would ever end. That was the scariest thought. She didn't let herself think on that too much. She wanted to always have hope that things would turn out good for her so that she could end hell for all her brothers and sisters.

Mama said getting a divorce would send you to hell, as well as smoking a cigarette, drinking alcohol (even a beer), dancing, going to movies or watching television, getting a permanent, wearing short skirts, mixed bathing (swimming), cussing in church, and taking God's Name in vain.

Cheryl figured Mr. McGinnis would go to hell for the things he did to her. Logic would conclude that Mama would be destined for hell too, but Cheryl didn't like to think about that. Besides, Mama wasn't a direct participant. Mama had other men over when Daddy was in prison and when Daddy was gone, but she never let a divorced man near her.

Even now that Daddy was out of prison, Rev. Hyatt would sometimes come and spend the night during the week when Daddy was out of town. Daddy was gone out on construction jobs many times during the week and would come home only on the weekends. Whenever Rev. Hyatt held a revival, Mama would go sit through the whole thing. All the children had to go too and listen to every word. Cheryl hated him. She knew it was wrong, but she couldn't stop the feelings. He would pace up and down the wooden platform thumping his Bible, sweating and spitting, red-faced, and mopping his forehead with a white handkerchief as he shouted his sermon at the top of his lungs.

Toward the end of the evening, exhausted and hoarse, he would make the altar call with his wife singing at least fourteen verses of "Just as I Am." Sometimes his wife didn't come along and Mama would sing the "Just as I Am." Cheryl wanted to respond to every altar call. She always felt condemned for her love/hate relationship with Mama and never felt that she measured up to what Jesus wanted from her.

There were the visits to Mr. McGinnis and other men to contend with. There was the constant struggle between being an obedient and respectful child for Mama as was commanded in the Bible, and yet allowing the men to touch her and hurt her in a way she knew had to be wrong, even though Mama required it of her. The first time Rev. Hyatt had come to the house, she thought she might be able to ask him some of these nagging questions, but it was immediately clear that his interest was in Mama. Watching Rev. Hyatt climb all over Mama, Cheryl vowed that when she grew up she would never attend a church in his denomination.

She thought a different type church might be better, so she persuaded Mama to let them go on a different church bus. This caused further confusion for Cheryl. She became especially upset upon hearing a sermon from the new minister where the children were bussed on Sundays. He preached that anyone who "touched the anointed" (meaning preachers) would be hell-bound for sure. He also said that if a preacher hooked up with a harlot (that was, anyone not his wife) he would be hell- bound too, and in real trouble with God. After that, Cheryl was very nervous whenever Rev. Hyatt came to visit. She could never relax until he was gone.

Once Mama had confided a dream to Cheryl. She said she'd dreamed that Rev. and Mrs. Hyatt were in a terrible car wreck and Mrs. Hyatt was killed, but Rev. Hyatt had survived. On the same day, she divulged that she dreamed she and Daddy were in a car accident too and Daddy was killed, but all the children and Mama survived. Mama said that then she and Rev. Hyatt got married and lived happily ever after with her six children and his three children and one child of their own.

"Would you like that, Cheryl?" Cheryl wasn't sure how to respond. She couldn't be truthful about her feelings toward Rev. Hyatt. She also didn't like the idea of Daddy being killed in a car wreck. The only portion of the dream she liked was a new baby. Kari was almost four now. "That would be just fine if we got a new baby, Mama," she answered half-truthfully.

"You're weird, Cheryl, really weird." With that the confidant session was over. Cheryl worried about Daddy and Rev. Hyatt. She hoped the dream never came true. It might, though. Sometimes it seemed Mama had strange powers like that.

* * *

They were at school now and the bell was already ringing. "Run to your classes," Cheryl instructed the others. "Meet me here on the steps at lunch times and we'll walk home together." Cheryl ran up the stairs, and taking a deep breath, opened the door and walked in.

"You're late again, Cheryl Morgan," Mrs. Bates said, not bothering to look up.

"I'm sorry. I won't be late again." Cheryl gave her usual response.

"If you are, you will be writing one hundred sentences and I will have to send you to the principal's office. Take your seat." Mrs. Bates looked up, and for the first time noticed Cheryl's dirty, tear-streaked face and her fresh haircut. "Well," she said, "it's about time someone cut off that unruly mane of yours. It looks… better, Cheryl."

Wearing a pink wool sweater (that had once been an adult size accidentally shrunken down to child size), Cheryl felt very dressed up. It had little pastel flowers sewn on around the neckline. With it she wore a red felt circle skirt. This too had belonged to an adult, but Cheryl had rolled it up at the waist until it was about the right length. It left a telltale bulge under the sweater, but she didn't mind. Robbin leaned over and said, "Stupid, don't you know that red and pink are clashing colors? No one wears red and pink together." Cheryl didn't know, but retorted, "Well, they do now."

Everyone lined up at the door and one by one sat down in the chair in front of the camera. Mrs. Bates smoothed everyone's hair and adjusted their clothing just before they were seated for the photographer. When it came Cheryl's turn, Mrs. Bates surveyed her and told her, "You look fine, dear. Smile." With her picture taken Cheryl got up to return to the classroom. Robbin leaned over so her ponytail fell forward. "Your hair is a mess. Mrs. Bates just didn't want to get lice in her brush." Cheryl kicked her shin, ran into the classroom and quickly buried her face in a textbook.

At lunchtime Mrs. Bates warned, "Cheryl, you'd better be back from lunch on time or you'll be in real trouble." She hurried out the door to meet her brothers and sister. When it was really cold and there was deep snow they all ate the free lunch program at school. Otherwise they ran home for lunch – partially so she could perform little chores for Bea, but also to play with Kari and break up her day. It made Cheryl uneasy leaving Kari alone with Mama all day. Mama slept too much and she was afraid something bad might happen to Kari.

They all raced home and Cheryl quickly made peanut butter sandwiches and Kool-Aid for everyone. She gathered the laundry from the clothesline and hung out another load. Grabbing a sweater and kissing Kari goodbye, she hurried out the door with the other children. "We have to run all the way or we'll be late. Hurry!"

The bell was ringing when they reached the steps. Cheryl knew she was already in trouble, so she took her time getting inside the building and going upstairs. She opened the classroom door and stood in the doorway ready to pivot around and be marched to the principal's office. Mrs. Bates was advancing toward her looking very annoyed.

Suddenly the loudspeaker came on. The principal was speaking and asking for everyone's attention. Mrs. Bates motioned Cheryl to sit down. She listened as the principal's voice, sounding very grave, delivered the startling news.

"President John Fitzgerald Kennedy is dead. He was shot down by an assassin's bullet in Dallas, Texas, today. School will be dismissed for the rest of the day. All children are to go home immediately. The mayor has ordered all flags in the city on Main Street to fly at half-mast. There will be a prayer meeting tonight held at City Hall for our country and the Kennedy family. You are dismissed."

All the children were dazed. Kennedy was almost like God in the state of South Dakota. Most of Cheryl's schoolmates were

Catholic. As they dispersed and began walking home, the children talked little among themselves. Everyone was afraid and wanted to get home. Robbin looked frightened as she hurried past Cheryl. "The Communists are going to take over America now, Cheryl. There's going to be a world war," she stated with certainty. A chill spread over Cheryl.

As they walked down Main Street toward home she saw the workers were already lowering the flags. People were standing in their shop doorways talking in low voices, crying and shaking their heads. Cheryl picked up her pace. She needed to get herself and the kids back home to Kari and Mama before war broke out. She hoped Daddy was headed back home from wherever he was. Mama motioned the children to be quiet as they burst in the front door. The radio from her bedroom was on the kitchen table and Mama sat listening, bent forward, her head cocked toward the speaker. A soggy wad of tissue was clutched in one hand, and she wiped her eyes with another wad.

The children gathered close, edging as near to Mama as they dared without touching her, to offer their comfort. They all listened in dismay and disbelief as the radio announcers gave details of the monstrous tragedy and national loss with the assassination of the President of the United States. Fright filled the hearts and minds of children and adults alike as the world watched and listened the next few days until Kennedy was buried.

It was so shocking to Cheryl that even the President wasn't safe. She felt very sorry for little Caroline and John-John because they had lost their wonderful daddy. At school the teacher had made a collage of the Kennedy family on a bulletin board. Cheryl's favorite pictures were one of Caroline sitting on her Mama's lap biting her pearls and another of Caroline on a tricycle in her daddy's office. They always looked so happy. Cheryl could tell that Caroline had no fear in her eyes. It must have been a wonderful life. She wondered what would happen to Mrs. Kennedy. They'd probably get thrown out of the White House since Mr. Lyndon Baines Johnson was taking over. She was afraid for the Kennedys. The murderer might come after them, too.

Mama finally turned off the radio and stood up. "I have to go lie down," she said, blowing her nose. "Bring me some water to take my nerve medicine with." Motioning the other children to stay put, Cheryl got the water and tiptoed into Mama's bedroom.

"Are you okay, Mama?"

"Yes, I'm just so upset over the assassination of the President. It's the Communists, you know. Poor Jacqueline, left with those two kids. You know, we look a lot alike. If I'd stayed with Aunt Frances instead of marrying your daddy, I might have married Jack Kennedy. With the right clothes and enough money to get into the right social circles I could have really been somebody." Mama had taken the nerve medicine and was leaned back propped up on pillows, talking more to the air than to Cheryl.

"Your daddy lied to me! He told me his parents were rich. He told me he would buy me anything I wanted. He said we would live in a big white house with white pillars and a maid. He told me he'd buy me a convertible car in any color I wanted. And diamonds, he told me he'd buy me diamonds. All I ever got out of him was this thin, cheap white gold wedding band and six lousy kids."

Cheryl prayed the medicine would kick in and Mama would

161

drift off to sleep before she got too angry. She ventured, "Mama, you better close your eyes now. You know that medicine makes you woozy."

Mama appeared not to hear. "All I ever got from him was lies. Lies, lies, lies. Here I am stuck here with you kids day in and day out. I don't have any money. I don't have pretty things. I don't live in a nice house, and I've only got a beat-up, second-hand Chevy. At least Jacqueline Kennedy got to have money and power, beautiful clothes and attention. The whole world loves her. Look at me! Even I am crying for her. I don't really feel sorry for her. I want to be her. I should be her! I hate her. Why am I crying for her? She'll be pampered the rest of her life. I don't have anything. I don't even have a friend or a sister. At least if I had a sister I'd have someone to talk to. Jacqueline Kennedy has a sister. I'm so alone, so isolated."

Mama sat up in the bed and put her arms around an imaginary Jacqueline Kennedy. "There, there, darling. Everything will be okay." She threw her hands up in the air. "That's what they'll say alright. 'Poor little widow. Left alone with those two little children. She's so young. Poor thing.' Look at me! I'm left alone with six little children. Nobody cares about me. My mother is dead and I'm glad. I hated that woman. I hope she's rotting in hell. I don't even know where my worthless father is."

Mama started to cry again. "You know, Cheryl, I never even saw my father. He's probably having a gay old time living it up somewhere never even remembering he has a son and a daughter. Do you think he ever wonders about me?" Mama looked very sad. "I'm sure he does, Mama. Why, I'll bet he thinks about you every day. He probably looks at ladies going down the street and wonders if one of them is you." Cheryl hoped she could comfort her mother.

"Oh, shut up. You're so ignorant. You don't know anything. If he'd ever thought of me he'd have found me by now. For God sakes, Cheryl, my mother had eleven sisters and he knew every one of them. He didn't want me or care about me then, he sure as hell doesn't now. Get out of here. Leave me alone." She waved Cheryl toward the door.

Cheryl dared to approach her mother. She could sense her vulnerability in that moment. "Mama, I can be your friend or we could pretend I'm your sister. Some people have big sisters that are seventeen and eighteen years older than them."

"You idiot, you can't be my friend or my little sister. How could I forget that you're my daughter? You can't understand grown-up things anyway. You want to hear some problems that I would talk to a sister or girlfriend about? Okay, listen to this. I hate myself. I hate my life. I hate my husband. I hate my children. I love my children. My life is a failure. After staying married to my husband while he had an easy life in prison, he comes home to me and still runs off and leaves me all week saddled with six kids. To top it off, he's impotent and God only knows how, but I think I'm pregnant again. The bill collectors are ringing the phone off the wall and banging on the door every day.

"I was destined to live a rich and pampered life, and to be famous and dressed beautifully and waited on hand and foot. I could have been a famous singer, you know. I have a good, strong voice and a wide range. I wouldn't even need a microphone. Instead, I have six dirty, stinking, ungrateful kids, a no good day-dreaming jailbird husband who can't come to bed without a stack of pornography, and a mother and father-in-law who blame me for everything bad that happens to him or you kids. Why, they think it's even my fault he went to jail!

"Now, little Miss Smarty-Pants, I can be your friend/big sister, you know so much... How do you propose I handle this so that I don't go off the deep end and kill myself and my kids in the process? Huh? Answer me!"

Leaping off the bed, she grabbed Cheryl's throat and shook her. "Answer me!" The effort it took to unload emotionally and the effect of the medications seemed to almost instantly take hold and Mama collapsed onto the floor. Cheryl helped her to the bed.

After gathering the discarded, ragged tissues and covering Mama, she reached over and put a clean tissue in her hand. Tip-toeing backward from the room, she quietly pulled the door shut and went in to feed the other children.

Cheryl felt sorry for Mama. Perhaps it was all the anger and remorse over the way her life had turned out that caused Mama to be so mean sometimes. Cheryl figured that if she had that much unhappiness stuffed down inside her heart she'd probably take her unhappiness out on anybody she dared. If she could figure out a way to make Mama happy, then maybe Mama wouldn't beat the children so much. It was an idea certainly worth considerable effort. Cheryl was in the fourth grade now and was learning a lot more about life. Maybe she'd learn something to help Mama.

Daddy did come home the next day and his being there seemed to soothe Mama. He assured the children that there wasn't going to be a war just because President John Fitzgerald Kennedy got knocked off. The funeral service was to broadcast over television. Mama wouldn't allow a television in the house. She said it was a "devil's box." Daddy wasn't interested one bit in seeing the funeral. He saw it as an excellent opportunity to make sales.

Unloading a big box from the trunk of the car, he showed the children things he was going to have them sell. There were necklaces, earrings, billfolds, ink pens and salve in a little tin can for minor skin abrasions. With everyone home watching the funeral Daddy figured the children could make a lot of sales.

He was right, too. People didn't want to be torn away from their television screens for long. Almost without exception they would absently purchase an item just to be rid of the kids and get back to the tiny screen.

Cheryl wished Mama would get over being scared of televisions. She went to church more than Mama did and had never read anything in the Bible that indicated television would damn a soul to hell.

Soon it was Christmas again and Mama was in the hospital. Daddy said they were scraping her insides because she had miscarried the baby. Grandma Morgan came and stayed a few days filling the house with the smell of Pine-Sol, Comet, Clorox and chocolate chip cookies. For Daddy she made mince meat pies. The children were invited to try a piece but declined. The dark filling, odd aroma, the unidentifiable minuscule bits making up the filling combined with the word "meat" for a sweet pie seemed too strange to risk. With wrinkled noses they opted for the known pleasures of Grandma's creamed potatoes, green pea salad, meat loaf, biscuits and cookies.

It was a splendid sensation to go to bed feeling full, warm and satisfied. Grandma had explained to the children that God had taken the baby to heaven because there was something wrong with it that wouldn't have allowed it to live in health in this world. Cheryl understood that the baby was better off with God and the angels in heaven, but it made her sad to think the baby had faced death being so tiny and helpless.

Mama came home looking very tired, thin and pale. Grandma Morgan went back home and Daddy and the kids began packing. Some men had been by the day before to talk to Daddy. Though he talked to them outside where the children couldn't hear, Cheryl knew they'd made Daddy nervous. She could see his heavy, nervous breathing rising in tiny, agitated visible wisps drifting in the frosty air.

When Mama came home he told the children that Mama wanted to move because the house made her sad over the "lost" baby. Privately Cheryl doubted the move had anything to do with the loss of the baby. More than likely it had to be connected to Daddy's visit from the two men. Though they weren't in uniform, she'd sensed they were policemen.

They moved to a town not far away and were settled in when school started again after the New Year's holiday. Cheryl registered everyone in school the first day, rattling off names, ages, birthdates, immunizations and previous school attended for herself, Davey, Richie, Eddie and Kati.

Next fall Kari would get to start school. That would be a big relief for Cheryl. She figured it might help Mama too. Maybe having a break from all the kids would help her get better. Cheryl pledged to herself and her friend Jesus to do all in her power to work harder at pleasing Mama and helping her more. Occasionally Cheryl would lapse into self-pity herself and get mad at Mama for being sick and sad and having a nervous condition. She resented Mama for not measuring up and not babying her or the other children every once in a while. Mama was a selfish person and sometimes Cheryl didn't even like her.

Those feelings made her feel guilty. After all, she was partially responsible for Mama's unhappiness. If Mama hadn't gotten pregnant with her in the first place, perhaps she could have been Mrs. John F. Kennedy, or at least someone of importance. She knew it wasn't good for her or the other kids to allow bad thoughts toward Mama. Following her "poor me" moments, Cheryl would renew her pledge to please and assist Mama. She was exactly right about her gestures of care and service toward Mama. It produced some brief, peaceful periods for Cheryl and the other children.

TWELVE

If a compass were positioned on a map at the location where South Dakota, Nebraska and Iowa all come together and then it was swiveled to create a circle, this would give a picture of most of the towns the Morgan family wandered over the course of the next two to three years. The average length of residence in a particular town was three months. They were almost transient, moving in the night hours, swiftly and silently to a new location.

The reasons for moving were as numerous as the moves. Sometimes it was because one of the children was in trouble at school. Often Bea would pick a fight with neighbors and emotions would escalate until the situation was intolerable. Other times people in the community, schools or churches would take note of the evidences of neglect and abuse exposed on the children by tell-tale bruises, wounds, injuries and excessive absenteeism. The disturbing symptoms prompted much talk, speculation and curiosity, but little action.

Most often it was because Renny got himself into difficult

scrapes with the law for exposing himself. He was also repeatedly reported for showing pornographic materials to minor girls in his car and at parks. The small towns he migrated to usually had only one or two law men, ill equipped to deal with Renny's problems. Typically he was considered relatively harmless anyway. With quite a line of pornographic literature to sell, trade and share, Renny gave up legitimate employment and opted for the more lucrative and migratory field of pornography sales, promotion of nudist colonies and "get rich quick" schemes. In the small Midwestern towns all he had to do was move into the next county to avoid prosecution.

One particularly profitable scheme caused many heated arguments between Renny and Bea. Renny would scan area newspapers for miles around and collect names and addresses from the obituaries. He had a little foil stamper and would print the name of the "deceased" person's spouse on a Bible. A short time after the funeral he would appear at the "survivor's" door with the personalized Bible... and a bill. Renny would tell the bereaved mate that the Bible had been secretly ordered as a surprise gift for them from their recently departed, dearly beloved. Of course, the poor soul would eagerly accept and gladly pay for the Bible without question. It was always a sure sale.

Bea was extremely nervous about the scheme. She felt very ill at ease using the Bible to profit, and especially using the obituaries to select "clients." Renny was constantly reassuring her that God wouldn't be angry about it. It was a justifiable means of earning an income that would help support her and all those kids. No regular job would enable them to have as good an income for the time, especially with that many kids and no real education or special training. Bea also began to despise the pornography. It was beginning to consume every realm of their existence. Immersed in it were the children, Renny, herself and even the family pets.

Continually tense about the law and under stress mentally, financially, physically and emotionally, Bea collapsed with another "nervous breakdown" and spent a few weeks in the state asylum. Renny convinced Bea that he would decrease the legal risks they were taking by dealing directly only with contacts he could trust. He promised to take on some "legal" sales jobs that would lessen the prying of outsiders concerning Renny's occupation and the source of income.

When Bea was released from the asylum, Renny promised her a house in the country. Evading their current landlord, Renny moved out in the night again. With the money meant for past rent he found a little farm to rent in Nebraska.

The move still meant Renny was usually gone during the week and home on the weekends. The children dreaded Renny's coming home. Bea would punish them during the week, but in addition would save up a list of offenses for Renny. Every Friday night upon his arrival, Bea would present him with the list. Lining the children up against the wall he would noisily recite each offense and offer punishment.

For Cheryl his "sentences" included humiliation, kicking in the stomach and ribs, and blows from the belt. Though he never hit as long or as hard as Mama, and never drew blood, Renny's blows were almost always delivered to bare skin, usually across the chest and pelvic area. For verbal offenses such as back talk or disrespect he would soap and pepper the tongue with cayenne pepper and strike her mouth with a belt.

Davey learned to jump and scream and holler at the slightest touch and seemed to escape the more brutal beatings from Bea, but Renny was perhaps the hardest on him and on Richie.

One time Renny caught Davey looking some of his pornographic magazines. As punishment Renny lined up the other children to watch, then stripped Davey. He had him lie down, face up and nude on the floor. Then, with a belt, beat him in the pelvic area until he drew blood. Davey was about twelve years old at that beating. Though the other children were not physically harmed by the incident, it was a horrifying experience for them to witness. Cheryl closed her eyes and tried to shut out the images of his suffering and the sound of his screams.

After that incident Davey seemed to harden to pain more than ever. He also began to get into trouble at school. Renny would pick him up by the neck, pound his head against the wall, stomp and kick him, beat him with his fists, and verbally butcher Davey. He began running away from home and established a pattern of running away and coming back. Davey started helping his father in minor illegal schemes just to be with him and seek his approval. Tough life "on the road" caused him to drop out of school, take up smoking, drugs and drinking. Soon minor legal scrapes such as hitchhiking, charges of running away, vagrancy, petty thievery, and under-age drinking escalated into stealing automobiles, buying and selling drugs, and just "being in the wrong place at the wrong time with the wrong people."

Renny let it be known to Davey, Bea, and the other children

and the authorities that he did not intend to spend one dime on a defense for Davey. So, Renny and Bea's oldest son was left to the mercy of courts and court-appointed attorneys, paid little money with little or no interest in Davey or his difficulties.

Davey never purposefully set out to do anything illegal. Usually the crimes he committed simply meant survival for him. His crimes in the beginning were motivated by either hunger and self-preservation, or an attempt to please his father. Davey's self-esteem and value were so eroded that he seemed on a deliberate path of self-destruction. Had he felt loved and valued, his life could have been so very different.

He was a good singer. Davey had a good, strong, resonant voice. He was compassionate and friendly. He never met a stranger and trusted and valued everyone he met. Financial resources (or lack of them), physical appearance, bums, businesspersons, young, old, male, female, none of these attributes mattered to him. If Davey knew a person, whatever Davey had was theirs, freely given, with no expectations or strings attached.

Davey would give his last dollar to a stranger he felt needed it. That person would never know that Davey might not have dinner or even a bed to sleep in himself. He kept reality clouded with drugs and alcohol when he wasn't in prison. In prison he was forced to be introspective and wrote long letters and poems sent most frequently to his sister Cheryl and his mother. Along with the letters and poems he usually sent elaborate drawings typically loosely based upon something spiritual.

In prison Davey got his G.E.D. and a mechanic's license. He also took several other courses that further educated him. If

Davey could have had a dream situation he would have been a carpenter of beautiful and intricate pieces of furniture by day and a well-known and loved disc jockey by night. Those dreams remained only dreams because alcohol had such a tight grip on him. He couldn't loosen the bands long enough to break through to reality.

Grandpa Morgan recognized the value in Davey and often said, "Davey is a good boy, and he has a good heart. If that boy had a dad who spent time with him he wouldn't have ever been in trouble."

Cheryl's most fervent prayer for Davey after she left home was that some older man would come into his life to mentor him, take an interest in him, and restore to him his self-worth and value.

After several destructive relationships with women, Davey married a rough older woman with three children. She was abusive to him and he eventually left her. Another long-standing relationship was with an alcoholic woman. She and Davey hitchhiked cross-country, stopping to savor local bars. This woman was a very angry person and would throw knives, canned goods and her fists at Davey. He finally listened to his sisters, and one night as she lay in a drunken stupor, he walked out of her life.

Davey ended up in prison again, this time in Arizona. With another year to go before parole, Cheryl, Eddie and Kari came to visit him. They told him Bea was terminally ill with cancer. By that time, all the children were grown and Renny and Bea were divorced. The authorities had agreed to allow Davey a few hours away from the prison. They said he would have to go in shackles and handcuffs with two uniformed officers and he had to choose either a two-hour visit with Bea now, or privileges to attend her funeral. He would not be allowed to do both. Davey chose the two-hour visit with his mother while she was still living.

Information given, medical verification provided, and forms filled out, the other siblings journeyed back to the hospital. Two days later Davey was escorted into the hospital. No one ever found out why, but Davey was dressed in street clothes with one plain-clothes police officer, and he was not in shackles or handcuffs. The officer also waited in the hallway and let the young man make his final visit with his mother in privacy.

Davey felt he had nothing he could give his mother. Despite the hurts of his childhood, Davey, like the others, loved his mother. He had drawn a rose on a small piece of paper, and in carefully penned words, had written her a poem. Both Bea and Davey were overcome with emotion and couldn't speak. They hadn't seen each other in two years.

Davey stood at the base of his mother's hospital bed with tear-brimmed eyes as Cheryl read his poem to Bea. Bea, unable to rise up, locked her gaze on him. She too was fighting tears. Though everyone knew this was likely the last time they would ever see each other in this life, no one wanted to say it out loud.

Cheryl finished reading the poem and carefully folded it back into the tiny envelope Davey had made for it. She tucked it into Bea's bony hand and closed her fingers around it. Bea reached her hand out to Davey and summoned strength to speak, "Thank you, Davey... it's a beautiful poem, a wonderful gift."

Davey moved to take her hand then leaned down to kiss her on the cheek. "I have to go, Mama. I love you." He could hold back the tears no longer.

"I love you, Davey. Goodbye." Bea was crying too.

Davey turned and walked slowly out the door. He felt so out of control. Because of his sentence for his wrongdoing he couldn't even be free to be with his mother her last few days on this earth. He was overwhelmed with sorrow. It was such a bitter blow. It had never mattered to him before that much if he was in jail or not. Now he wanted to be out, and stay out. Until the point of her death he really had not considered that he cared that greatly for his mother. It seemed that her impending death erased a great deal of the anger and bitterness he held against her.

A year later, when he was released, Davey vowed that he would never be involved in any wrongdoing that could send him to a penitentiary. He did have a battle with alcohol and spent many nights in the "drunk tank" of the city jails wherever he lived. His inability to be with his mother when she died and being prevented from attending her funeral had a permanent effect on his behavior. He was never again as self-destructive of his own life after her death.

Two years after her death he had been out of prison for a year and then married for a year. Six years after being released from prison he was still married to Sula. Not only did they have her two children from a previous marriage, but also they had a son, Little Davey, and a set of twins – a boy and a girl. Davey thrived in a family environment and settled into a regular job. He joined Alcoholics Anonymous to get free from his persistent problem with drinking. It helped him cut back, but he still went on periodic binges.

Even after so many years, he still didn't like thinking about his childhood. Cheryl pressed him to talk about it, but he wanted to just forget it. He couldn't change anything anyway. He still wanted Renny's approval. Renny was very irate about the kids all talking about their "abusive childhood." He would say defensively, "I did the best I could, and I had a lot of responsibility." Renny felt Cheryl and Eddie had it in for him and were just trying to stir up trouble in the family. Besides, Bea was dead; she couldn't defend herself. Of course, it was all lies anyway. Every one of those lousy kids was lying.

Renny couldn't understand it. He'd done the best he could for them. They were just ungrateful. Sure, he was a little hard on them, but hey, he had been very young when he had seven mouths to feed. They just couldn't seem to grasp how hard it had been for him. Eddie was just mad because he'd gotten in legal trouble and he was going to punish Renny for it. Renny told Davey, "That crazy psychiatrist is just stirring up your brother. He just wants his money. He doesn't give a hoot about Eddie. He just wants his money. He's using some mind games on him. Those things never happened. You understand how it really was, don't you, Davey?"

Davey answered in the affirmative, but he had his doubts. He didn't like to think about his childhood. Richie, Eddie and Cheryl had been pumping him full of information and he was beginning to remember a lot of things that he didn't like to think about. But, there was a little advantage to this. Renny was talking to him. Renny was on his side. Renny was treating Davey like a buddy. Davey didn't like some of the memories that were nudging their way to the surface anyway. He decided he'd just squelch them back down. Who needed to remember all that garbage anyway?

* * *

Eddie didn't feel that way. He was spending hours every day writing in private journals. Notebooks were filling up with his memories. As he'd write out one incident in detail, a dozen more would come flooding into his memory.

Before he had reached his teen years, Eddie had long since steeled himself against the abuses and endured any punishment almost serenely. He mutely endured pain, though a slight glimmer of suffering and hurt flashing fleetingly in his eyes was noticeable to a careful observer like Cheryl.

Eddie's inner rage and anger was acted out coldly and cruelly to animals. He would stomp mice, blow up frogs with firecrackers, dip cats' tails in gasoline and light them. He had watched emotionless as the cats bolted frantically, screaming to get away from the anguish and pain of their burning flesh, until finally they would drop over in smoldering heaps. The only other compelling force in Eddie's life besides death and destruction was his appetite for wealth and "the finer things in life." By junior high school, older, pedophile "friends" fed upon that greed. They "wined and dined" him, educated him, and created in him a penchant for travel, antiques and other valuable collectibles.

Ironically, it was a charge of molestation against Eddie that was the impetus to legally force him to get professional psychiatric help. By that time he was in his thirties and had much to overcome. His saving grace was that he had sporadically kept involved in churches. Because of that he had hope. He had hope that perhaps his life might be worth living.

Many times during the years of intensive therapy he would descend into bouts of deep depression. Cheryl frequently feared for his life, apprehensive that he might attempt suicide. During those times she would flood the mail cross-country with cards and notes and little gifts of encouragement. His physiatrist had specialized in dealing with abuse for over twenty years and alleged that Eddie's case was the worst he'd ever dealt with.

Eddie's appetite for riches served to motivate him to continue writing. He was sure he would sell his story and finally make his million dollars. Wouldn't that be an ironic twist -- he could achieve what his father and mother had desired all their lives by exposing their evil. Eddie relished the thought. Meanwhile, he started a remodeling business, and in a very practical way worked toward making his dream of financial freedom become a reality.

* * *

Richie had always been quite small for his age. Perhaps it was because he was a little "runt" that Cheryl felt most protective of him. More likely, though, it was a kindred spirit. Both Richie and Cheryl were survivors with very strong spirits. They were a great source of comfort to one another.

Cheryl was the oldest child; Richie was the fourth child and the youngest boy. They could never quite ascertain the logic for it, but it seemed that they were the most often ill treated and most severely beaten of the children. Conceivably their unique closeness and loyalty to each other irritated their parents. Sometimes Bea would test their loyalty by requiring one to take a beating for the other. Cheryl offered herself in Richie's stead as often as her own physical condition would allow. Richie seemed so small and she could scarcely bear to hear him scream in pain and terror.

Renny appeared to be furious with Richie almost constantly. Though he knew Bea beat Richie often and severely, he was very brutal in his weekend discipline. Richie looked the most like his mother with flashing brown/black eyes and black hair. His fair skin was like Renny's and his face was freckled. The contrast annoyed Renny.

He liked to intimidate Richie. Bending down and thrusting his finger hard into Richie's chest, Renny would back him into a corner and yell and taunt, jeer at, ridicule and humiliate Richie to the point of tears. He would tell him he was a useless creature and someday he was going to kill him. He would then raise Richie off the ground and choke him until he lost consciousness. When Richie would awaken, Renny would be right back in his face, laughing. "Next time, I'll choke you a little longer. You were lucky. You made it this time, but maybe next time you won't." Then he'd kick him again and walk away laughing.

The most experienced military man could not have plotted or devised more complex assassination attempts than Richie. In the night hours his mind would conceive various methods to murder Renny and Bea. For what seemed hours some nights, he would lie in bed, sweating, striving to conquer his overwhelming fear of them. He so wished he could work up the nerve to simply rise from the bed and carry out one of his intricate schemes. Richie wasn't alone in those angry thoughts. On any given night there might be several murderous little pounding hearts aspiring to conquer their fears and rise up to destroy the source of that fear, their own parents.

To most young men, especially at sixteen, life in the Navy would have been a harsh contrast for them. For Richie it was a wondrous thing to have a bed to sleep in every night, three meals a day, money to spend, and some fun times of laughter and play with his buddies. Since he had begun running away from home at age eleven, life in the Navy was a life of comfort, plenty, and contentment, and -- at the very least -- safety.

Though he had gotten involved in drugs and alcohol, Richie got free of all those crutches when loving people in a little Pentecostal church in Virginia Beach filled the void in his life. It was there that he put his natural musical talents of singing and guitar playing to good use in the church band. A pretty, dark-haired guitar player caught his eye and the two were soon married. Richie stabilized with the love and support of his church, his wife, and soon one very special little girl, his daughter Krista.

The Navy had been his foster parent and he made a lifetime career out of what had been his haven of rest. His faith, time, physical distance and the death of Bea contributed to Richie's ability to forgive, forget and move on with his life. There were still scars, but he refused to allow his thought life to be dominated by all the lost, negative years.

* * *

Kati and Kari had a mutual loathing for Renny. Renny seemingly despised Kati. It really wasn't her he detested; it was what she represented. With her long blonde hair, her coke bottom thick glasses, she was a constant reminder of his and Bea's inability to control their anger. Because of her vision problems and her epileptic seizures, Renny and Bea dared not physically batter Kati much anymore. Renny had enough problems with the law, and Bea was terrified of being incarcerated. None of this stopped them from verbally persecuting Kati. She safeguarded herself with a dull shell of numbed emotions. She allowed herself no sorrow, grief or tears. It was a sub-conscious, self-prescribed cure for the never-ending powerlessness and hopelessness experienced by all the Morgan children.

Kari was three before she ever met Renny. Upon his release from prison he attempted to step right back into the home as if he'd never left. Kari resented his intrusion. His deep voice and towering frame frightened her. Constantly he was searching her features for any evidence of who her father might really be – himself or Rev. Hyatt. Kari sensed his spurning her and kept her distance for a long time. As she grew, though, she was a cute, petite blonde with tousled ringlets and wide blue eyes. She was dimply and friendly and people were attracted to her. Renny began to capitalize on her personality to lure people to him.

A vague memory of one of Renny's ex-con "friends" haunted Kari for years. She knew she was very small, probably about four or five and sitting on the lap of one of Renny's friends. Renny was in a chair opposite, with a clear view of the man holding Kari. She knew that under her dress the man was touching her in her private places as Renny watched. Shortly after that Renny had left her alone with the man. The sense of Renny's betrayal and lack of control over her own body caused Kari to carry a burdensome cargo of hatred and anger. It produced more destruction in her life as she grew up.

* * *

Cheryl left home at seventeen; Davey was gone off and on from the time he was fourteen. Eddie had stayed around until he graduated from high school, then he left and joined the Navy. Richie began running away from home at age eleven. Because of her vision problems, Kati never ran away physically, but she was recluse, withdrawn from everyone else for many years. She finally, through church, formed a friendship with an army man. They were soon married and within a few months had their first son. Two years later they had a second son.

When Kari was thirteen, Renny also left. During his week-long "sales trips" he had met and married someone else. It was bigamy, but no one found out about it for a few years. He left Bea just weeks before their 25th wedding anniversary. By then Bea had severe breathing problems, so she, Kari and Rosie moved to Arizona.

Kari lied about her age and took two jobs to support her mother and little sister. When those two jobs failed to provide enough money for them to live on, Kari took a third job. In order to function on only two to three hours of sleep per night, she began taking speed. Every payday she would hand her paychecks over to Bea, never even considering she should keep any of the money for herself. Bea, never in the habit of paying rent and utilities, usually squandered the money on expensive jewelry, clothing, or health clubs. Often they would be without utilities, living in an old beat-up car that Davey would scrounge up for them, or in a rat hole motel in a dangerous section of Phoenix.

After several months of working three jobs, Kari collapsed and was rushed to the hospital for an emergency appendectomy.

She abhorred being a "welfare case" in the ward at the hospital. In desperation she called Renny and asked for some financial assistance for Bea and Rosie. She told him about working the three jobs and having just gotten out of the hospital.

The electricity was off and there was no food in the house. Eviction from their apartment was inevitable. Renny coldly responded, "You need more money? Get another job. I'm not going to help you. As far as I'm concerned, you're not my daughter." Responding with a wounded heart, masked by a harsh voice, Kari said, "I have no father. I'll never call you again."

Knowing how upset and angry Bea would get upon every confrontation with Renny, Kari kept her conversation with him a secret. A few days later a money order from Renny for Bea in the amount of one hundred dollars arrived in the mail. Bea was happy with it, but it only served to harden Kari all the more toward Renny.

"Almost three years and he can only afford to send one hundred dollars to his wife and two daughters? I don't ever want to see or speak to him again," Kari declared.

Kari continued to help support her mother even after her own marriage. Her husband disapproved, so support was limited. It forced Bea to get a job. She took up crocheting for an exclusive designer and was able to earn a modest income. She also worked part time at a lingerie store at the mall.

Rosie, the seventh child and fourth daughter, had been born just ten months after Bea's miscarriage. She had a pampered upbringing compared to the standards the rest of the Morgan children lived with. Now that Renny was gone and Bea was sick, Rosie had gotten deeply involved in a large church and moved in with one of the pastors and his family as a nanny/housekeeper when she was seventeen.

Rosie had been removed from schooling in the second grade and Bea had sporadically home schooled her over the years. Consequently, at sixteen she was not able to function well socially. Her life from age seven to sixteen was a narrow, limited world of Renny, Bea, Kari, cats and soap operas.

As she got more involved in the church and socializing, Rosie became increasingly angry with Renny and Bea. Though she may have been "spoiled" in the estimation of the other children, in reality she had been "ruined" by Renny and Bea's indulgences. She was never beaten and had always been given the same food as her parents. If they went out to eat, Rosie always went with them. Rosie was the only child who had ever been photographed professionally, and consistently had new shoes and new clothing. It seemed to the other six children that she was treated as an only child and the other children were the slaves of her, Renny and Bea.

Their favoritism of Rosie generated dislike from her brothers and sisters. Being pulled out of school and socializing seemed to warp her. When she began to discover all she'd been robbed of with the supposed "princess" treatment, she too was embittered toward Renny and Bea.

When Bea was dying, Rosie made a token visit to the hospital upon the strong persistence, persuasion and insistence of Cheryl. She let it be known to Bea and the other children that Cheryl's insistence was the only reason she was there. Her visit was short and cold. It seemed that Rosie, who had the least to forgive, was the most unforgiving.

Cheryl pulled her aside and said imploringly, "Rosie, you've got to spend a little time with Mama. You'll be sorry later if you don't, then it will be too late. Right now the people you're living with seem enormously important, but someday they'll mean nothing to you. Blood is what matters. Your family will always be your family. This is your opportunity to connect with everyone, to make peace with Mama. It might be your last opportunity. Remember, you'll always have your family. Friends come and go, but blood family is always there."

"Well," said Rosie, "my friends are my family now, so I don't need you. I only went to see Mama because you pushed me. I didn't do it because I wanted to or felt a need to. You can't push me anymore. You can't make me visit her and you can't make me forgive her. If you need to, that's your business, but don't push your beliefs on me."

As Bea's body began to deteriorate, she suffered a massive coronary and was put on life support. Eddie called Rosie and said, "If you want to see Mama alive one more time, you'd better come now." Rosie's callous response was, "I'm too busy. I'll come to the funeral when she dies."

At the funeral the other children observed that she never shed a tear. In fact, she smiled through the whole service. Refusing to sit with the family, she surrounded herself with her own friends. She quickly left at the end of the formal service, declining to attend graveside rites.

Kati, living on the east coast with her husband and two boys, did not have enough money to return to visit Bea or attend the funeral. Cheryl and Kari offered to pay her way, but Kati refused. She wanted the entire family to return together to Arizona. In reality, Cheryl and Kari would have had to scrape together enough just for Kati to come.

Cheryl had been living in Oklahoma and returned there the day before Bea died. She did not attend the funeral. After five trips to Arizona from Oklahoma in less than a year, she had returned home on a Wednesday night. Bea died Thursday morning, Maundy Thursday, right before Easter. Cheryl chose not to return for the funeral, a decision she later regretted.

"The boys" took over the funeral arrangements. Richie's touch was a tissue tucked into Mama's hand. For years Bea had kept an assortment of tissues around her. They were in her pockets and in her hand for her chronic "bronchitis." Mistaking her continually worsening breathing problems for another bout with bronchitis, Bea had multiple tumors in both lungs before the cancer was discovered. Baffling the doctors, she lived almost another full year after their discovery of the cancer. Richie thought she just didn't look like herself without a tissue.

There was much arguing about how the headstone should read. It was kind of like trying to select a Father's Day card for Renny, or a Mother's Day card for Bea. They all said things that didn't fit, like "You were great," "To a wonderful dad," "To a loving mother," "You were always there for me"... Finally, with Bea laid to rest under a stone which simply read "Beloved Mother," the children scattered around the country.

One by one most gravitated to Minnesota where Renny was living with his third wife. Cheryl, Kari, Kati and Richie let the miles keep them separated, but first Rosie, then Davey, and then Eddie moved close to Renny. They picked up a relationship with him again as if the intervening years had never occurred.

Shortly after Bea's death, Kari's abusive husband continued to blatantly flaunt his girlfriends in front of her. One night she'd had enough. With her five-month-old son, she left Arizona for Oklahoma to live with Cheryl for a few months. When her husband followed her to Oklahoma and began to stalk her, she became terrified that he would kidnap her baby boy. He knew of Kari's contempt for Renny, and she believed Renny's was the last place her husband would search for her and the baby.

Swallowing her pride, fear of Renny, and her hatred for him, for the sake and safety of her child, she too moved to Minnesota. She stayed with Renny and his wife until she was able to get a job waitressing. As soon as she had enough money, she moved into a tiny apartment. It wasn't much, but at least she could rest at night without fear of Renny's perversions intruding on her. She was right. Her abusive husband never suspected she was in Minnesota with Renny. He soon gave up pestering Cheryl for Kari's whereabouts and moved back to Arizona.

Once she had established residency, Kari filed for divorce. Her attorney filed papers and had her husband served in Arizona. He did not contest the divorce. Though the divorce granted limited, supervised visitation to him and child support to Kari, neither ever happened. The baby's father never visited him and never paid child support. After almost two years, Kari began to relax.

Renny took on the personality of a loving father and doting grandfather. Though they didn't quite trust him yet, Davey, Eddie,

Rosie and Kari indulged him and began to include him in holiday gatherings. Cheryl and Richie would visit on major holidays and stay with Kari.

Finally, Kati and her family too moved to Minnesota to be near family. It seemed maybe they could be a normal family now that everyone was grown. Bea's death had taken the sharp edge out of their hatred. Without further agitation from Bea or Renny and no discussion among the siblings about how life had been when they lived at home, the reality of their upbringing began to fade. They so wanted to enjoy normal family relationships that they ignored a lot of evidences from Renny that he still was addicted to pornography and deviant behavior. That is, until it began to affect their own children.

Eddie's counseling and his and Cheryl's journals were both about to explode into the conscious and sub-conscious minds of all seven children. It was to be the end of a brief period of innocence and normality in their family life. Though the dredging up of all the horrible memories caused great pain for everyone, the end result was peace, healing and restoration for Cheryl, Davey, Eddie, Richie, Kati, Kari and Rosie.

Thirteen

Writing faithfully in her journal, Cheryl had pieced together much of her childhood. She was even able to help the other children remember bits and small incidents in their lives. It was distressing to them to have lost so much of their childhood. Even in remembering they couldn't be sure that what they remembered was really the truth. Their lives had been filled with so much lying, deception, betrayal and abuse that it was confusing to try to sort it all out.

Sometime around the seventh grade (for Cheryl) Mama had to let a "devils box" (television) in the house. Renny broke his ankle in a construction accident. With the crutches and cast he also brought home a television. The children were delighted. Mama refused to be in the same room with it at first, but she soon got use to it.

Mama's favorite shows were "Dark Shadows," "The Edge of Night," "The Secret Storm," and "The Guiding Light." With television the children didn't feel so isolated. Their restricted input from the outside world suddenly expanded beyond their imagination. Bea and Renny never watched sports or the news, but they watched everything else on television.

At least it got Bea out of the bed. She would sit all day in the recliner watching television. Though these were the days before remote control, Bea had seven little remote controllers at her beck and call. Watching television, she would sit and crochet or hold and stroke the Siamese cats or pedigreed toy poodles she raised. Often the children would observe her tenderly stroking the pets and wish they were animals instead of children. At least then Bea would have held and touched them.

Bea liked to have her long, dark hair brushed. She would have Cheryl, Eddie, Davey and Richie stand behind her chair for hours on end brushing her hair. Cheryl and Davey hated to brush Mama's hair. They made mean faces and raised the brush menacingly behind her back. Eddie and Richie would brush her hair the most. They seemed to last much longer before they tired. Cheryl and Davey ridiculed them for surrendering to Bea so apathetically.

Eddie and Richie maintained that they were much more cleverer than Cheryl and Davey. They knew that while they were brushing her hair they accomplished three things. First, they won favor with Mama for outlasting the others. Secondly, they were occupied with brushing her hair, thus received a reprieve from chores. Third, and most important of all, the hair brushing had a calming effect on Bea. When her hair was being brushed, she wasn't screaming, ranting and raving. She actually fell asleep sometimes. After the birth of Rosie, Renny and Bea lived in rental houses in rural areas. Renny had become much more sophisticated in his pornographic dealings. Living in the country provided a sheltered site to deal with customers because there were no prying neighbors to observe odd-hour visits. Another benefit was there was no one to overhear the anguished cries of pain from the children. Their isolation proved a powerful weapon to shatter the children's hopes of help from the outside.

Hank and Anna had only sporadic contact with them now that Renny was out of prison. With Renny, Bea, and the grandchildren no longer in South Dakota, Hank and Anna had sold their home and moved back to the hills of West Virginia.

Cheryl found that she too was growing up very cruel. Left in charge of the other children, sometimes for days at a time, she missed a lot of school. She resented the work she had to do and the responsibility. Though she never was nearly as cruel as Renny or Bea, she too began to beat her brothers and sisters with a belt. She hated it that she'd hit them or slap them and would try to love and comfort them afterward. Except for Eddie, they all seemed to be very forgiving toward her. Every time it happened and she "went out of control," she would vow it would never happen again. But it always did. The kids would fight or misbehave, or do something that was going to get her in trouble. There was no other way to control them. Once Renny and Bea (and usually Rosie) were out of the house, it seemed they all went berserk. Cheryl wondered if her whole life she would feel as irritable and angry as she did then.

Cheryl's teenage years passed in a blur. It seemed she was twelve and suddenly one day woke up and was sixteen. Everything in between, except fragmented pieces, was lost. She knew from being told that she had run away from home several times.

They moved constantly. They were involved with churches everywhere they went, and Bea began to attend fairly regularly. Renny would even attend at times. It didn't change how they acted, though. Mama could sing beautifully in church and look so pure and holy. She'd hug and shake hands and smile at all the church folks, then cuss and scream and holler and hit kids all the way home. It seemed even God couldn't control Mama and Daddy.

Even though she knew it was wrong, Cheryl would get exasperated, even enraged at God for not rescuing them. He'd witnessed their persecution for years. Why hadn't He done something to help them? At points of hopelessness there would always be some sign that would help renew her faith in God's ability to get them out of their circumstances. It would be just tiny things to anyone else -- a falling star, a dream, a scripture, a soothing hymn that would haunt her for days until she secured some peace. Her favorites were "Love Lifted Me" and "Victory in Jesus."

She'd hum the songs and say the words over and over again until "The Black" that was swallowing her up would lighten to gray. It seemed light would seep into her mind, her soul, her spirit, and briefly lift the heaviness. She'd silently sing the words to "Love Lifted Me":

"I was sinking deep in sin..." (Daddy and Mama's abuse, perversion, hatred, and cruelty)

"far from the peaceful shore..." (Of peace, love, worth, trust, childhood)

"Very deeply stained within..." (By powerlessness, hopelessness, vulnerability, betrayal, confusion, rejection, grief, malice, pornography, perversion, anger, bitterness, unforgiveness, condemnation, guilt, murderous hatred)

"And sinking to rise no more..." (Waiting to die, to escape, to run, to break out, be delivered, despairing at ever being able to rescue herself, much less the others).

"But the Master of the sea..." (God, Jesus, The Holy Spirit)

"Heard my despairing cry..." (It meant He could, He would, He could, He wanted to)

"And from the waters..." ("The Black")

" lifted me..." (And Davey and Eddie and Richie and Kati and Kari and Rosie)

"Now safe am I."

The chorus she would sing over and over until the words penetrated and became almost tangible... "Love lifted me, love lifted me, when NOTHING else could help, His love lifted me. Love lifted me. Loved lifted me. When nothing else COULD help, His love lifted me."

Singing the others to sleep, she would softly sing, "Oh, victory in Jesus, my Savior forever. He sought me and He bought me with His redeeming Blood. He loved me 'ere I knew Him, and all my love is due Him. He plunged me to victory beneath His cleansing blood."

Another escape from reality was a fantasy world that the kids would create every time they moved. Television helped to provide material for them to continually create new life histories for themselves. Since they were always attending new schools and usually lived isolated, out in the country, they could tell anything about themselves they wanted. Sometimes they would say they were from missionary parents. Other times they would say they had eccentric rich parents, paranoid that kidnappers were going to abduct their children (heirs) for ransom.

That would be the explanation for their poor dress despite their extreme wealth. Stories included a history of being "army brats" or children of gypsies. They didn't realize it at the time, but their real lives were much more bizarre than any fabrication they could imagine.

There were so many "holes" even in their collective memories. Cheryl had read that people deal with abuse in one of two ways. They either fragment into multiple personalities, or they block out hard memories creating "memory holes." It was a small blessing to consider that at least it appeared none of them had multiple personalities.

One persistent memory was an ongoing dream that Cheryl had been having ever since she was a small child. Periodically over the years she would have the dream again. It was always the same except every time she had it there was more to it. One night after she had been writing in the journal she had the same dream again. In reality, by now, she was a grown woman with a teenage son. She had experienced a remarkable healing process over the abuse and was already speaking publicly and frequently concerning "Victory Over Abuse."

The dream started out as always with a beautiful, but isolated, house that sat back, far from the main road. Only those who had been led to it even knew of its existence. On the outside it appeared to have two stories and to be well kept. On the inside, however, it was very ugly and torn up. It had obviously experienced severe destruction in the past and had never been mended, fixed, or cleaned up. There were holes in the walls. Pictures of her family were shattered.

There was garbage, trash, dead animals, broken furniture and dirty dishes everywhere. The beds were all broken and the mattresses rotting, torn and infested with mice and rats. It was treacherous to even walk across a room trying to avoid all the debris. Even though the floorboard looked safe and sturdy, it often gave way under her feet.

If, in the dream, one of her brothers or sisters were with her, they would always circle the entire house via a wrap-around porch and end up at the back, standing over a cellar door. Cheryl always opened the cellar door, but they never had the courage to walk down the cold, damp, dark steps into the darkness.

Though no sound came from the cellar, there were smells that seemed to surround and envelop them. The smells reminded them of fear and evil. They stirred negative emotions. Cheryl always smelled Sen-Sen and ether, burning flesh, animal waste, Mr. McGinnis' cigar, and men's sweat. They would hastily close the cellar door and run back to the front of the house.

They would always go into the house. Wandering through each time they would find a secret staircase that would lead to a hidden third floor. The third floor could not be detected from the outside. It seemed frightening because of the unknown, yet compelling at the same time. Every time Cheryl had the dream over the years, a new room would be discovered in the hidden third floor.

The rooms on the third floor were always clean, though dusty.

Faint light that came from everywhere illumined the rooms. It reminded Cheryl of a misty sunrise on a meadow in Georgia.

Each room on the third floor was totally different, yet the same. Each had beautiful, antique furnishings, with intricate carvings etched into the deep, rich woods. There were warm blue hues everywhere – in the wallpapers, the pillows, rugs and quilts. All the rooms were elaborately yet warmly and comfortably decorated. Everything that symbolized peace to Cheryl could be found in the rooms. There were Bibles (Cheryl often slept with a Bible) and pictures of Jesus, crosses, pictures of waterfalls, sunsets, rose gardens, fountains, and cathedrals.

Unseen music boxes played softly in all the rooms. In the dream Cheryl and whichever brother or sister was with her would be in awe at the splendor, beauty and serenity in the rooms on the third floor.

The dream was always disturbed in the same way. They would hear Renny and Bea shrieking at them to wake up, and Cheryl would awaken from the dream to discover it was again only a dream.

Throughout the years she felt that it must be a house she had once lived in or that it was a house she would someday find and buy to restore. It wasn't until she again had the dream after writing in the journal that she realized the meaning of the dream. It was in that dream that she dared to make the journey down the stairs to the cellar. It was then that the meaning of the dream became crystal clear.

The house symbolized Cheryl. The first two stories were her surface memories. The cellar represented the buried memories and the third, hidden floor, represented all that she and her brothers and sisters could become. She knew that once she went down into the cellar she would expose all the darkness there. The journal was going to be the beam of light that would uncover the darkness. Cheryl's faith and inner strength would be the power, the force behind the exposure that would enable all the children to confront the evils shrouded in the "cellar." Cheryl believed that perhaps just the exposure to the light would dissipate most of the darkness. Hopefully, the penetrating, illuminating light of confrontation would disintegrate and vanquish the trepidation associated with that darkness.

Though there were only very fragmented memories ever brought to her remembrance of her teenage years, Cheryl knew some facts about that time. Because of Renny and Bea's transient lifestyle, the whole family had to be ready to move at a moment's notice. There was virtually no material object, piece of furniture or clothing that could have much value, real or sentimental, because it would likely be left behind in a hasty move. Cheryl's life was so full of fantasy, lies and fabricated life stories that it became difficult to sort truth from fiction.

When she began writing the journal there had been years of healing time and peace in her life. It enabled her to begin to sort out the truth from lies. She learned to be very careful in what she wrote. Personal integrity was one of the most valuable things she possessed. She didn't want it tainted like the rest of her life had been. Being very careful to precisely record things that could be verified and confirmed by her brothers or sisters or documented by school, medical, and legal records was her safeguard against untruth.

One memory exposed was that shortly after her sixteenth birthday, Cheryl discovered her mother had been giving her "the pill" from the time she had begun menstruating. It made her furious with Bea. She didn't let her mother know that she discovered this deception. Instead she faked swallowing the little "female's vitamin" (as Bea had called it for years). Cheryl hoped she'd get pregnant and then she could escape Bea and get her own apartment and live with her little baby, happily ever after. One by one she'd move her younger brothers and sisters in with her.

Once in a great while Bea would get into a "buddy" mood with Cheryl and call her in to talk to her. It would usually be late on a Friday night, after Renny had called to announce that he was "going to stay out on the road for another week" before returning home. Bea liked to hold these little sessions in the bathroom with Cheryl sitting uncomfortably on the commode lid or the sink.

Bea would be soaking in the bathtub. Cheryl detested having to look at her mother's pale, naked body. Her body was distorted by the water, eight pregnancies, and a hysterectomy. They had left her sagging and heavy all over. Bea had no muscle tone from years of lounging in the bed, recliner, or sofa.

Cheryl swore she'd never get overweight, saggy and out of shape. Most of all, she'd be private with her body. Someday she'd have a choice about who would touch her, where, when, and for what reason. God had to have created sex to be more than just lying mute and passively on the surface while men panted and wheezed and sweat above women. Cheryl was sixteen now and an incident was about to take place that would set her free from the bondage of not having control over her own body.

It was a Sunday night and Renny, as usual, had left town to go "back out on the road" for the week. Bea decided she'd go to church and take the girls. Recently Renny had purchased a used black convertible for Bea to have transportation during the week. The upholstery and canvas top were a bit tattered, but Bea enjoyed it. Of course, when winter came it might be a little drafty, but she'd worry about that when the time came.

Davey, just out of the juvenile detention center again, and Eddie, studying for finals, elected to stay at home. No one knew where Richie was; he'd been gone for several months. So, Mama and "the girls" all went off to church. Mama drove and Cheryl sat in the front with four-year-old Rosie on her lap. Kati and Kari rode in the back. After church Mama stopped at a gas station to get a dollar's worth of gas and a Coke.

It was already dark and Mama didn't see well after dark. She pulled up too far, and putting the car in reverse, she accidently stepped on the gas pedal.

Lurching, the car jerked backward. The girls heard a thud, then a loud explosion.

Reeling around to see what they'd hit, Cheryl was shocked to see tall columns of raging fire shooting up behind the car. The flames were beginning to encircle the car. Mama had hit the gas pump.

"Mama, girls, get out! We're on fire!" Cheryl screamed. She pushed her door open, and half carrying, half dragging Rosie, got her to the curb. Racing back to the passenger side of the car, she pushed the seat forward to let Kari and Kati out of the back seat.

"Get out, hurry!" The door handles were already hot and the canvas top ablaze. Mama sat, frozen, her hands at the ten o'clock and two o'clock position on the steering wheel. Cheryl was pulling her immobilized little sisters from the car.

"Mama! Mama! Get out! The car's on fire! Get out now!" The little girls had run over to Rosie; the heat was forcing Cheryl to back away. Fire engines were wailing in the distance, getting closer. Cheryl was aware of other people running and yelling.

She ran around to the driver's side. Two men were already there trying to get Bea out. Cheryl pushed in between them and peeled Mama's hands off the steering wheel. "Hurry up, Mama! You're going to be burned alive!" The men got on either side of Bea and dragged her away from the burning car. By now the fire engines had pulled up and more men were running everywhere, yelling orders, dragging hoses, hollering back and forth.

All four girls were gathered around Mama as she began sobbing and shaking violently. She extended her hand toward the wildly burning car. "My nerve medicine. I've got to have my nerve medicine. It's in my purse. Cheryl, you have to get me my nerve medicine," Bea pleaded.

"Don't worry, Mama, I'll go get it." Cheryl ran toward the car. Firemen grabbed her and held her back.

"You can't get anything out of that car. It's going to blow any minute. We don't know when the gas tank will catch." The firemen held her back. Summoning extra strength, Cheryl broke free of the men and sprinted for the car. The door was still open. She reached in through the roaring flames and flying sparks, swiftly grabbed Mama's purse, and lunged back to safety. Mama was crying and screaming loudly. She clutched the purse close to her.

By now an ambulance had arrived. A police officer pulled Cheryl aside. "Honey, that wasn't a very smart thing to do. I'm glad you weren't hurt."

"I'm sorry, but you don't know my Mama. She will go crazy without her nerve medicine. I absolutely had to get it for her." Cheryl explained.

"Well, no offense, but I think your mother is a little crazy right now. I think I'll have the ambulance take her to the hospital, just to be on the safe side."

With that, the policeman summoned the ambulance driver over. Turning back to Cheryl, he said, "You and your sisters go ahead and ride in the ambulance with your mother. Is there someone that can come and get you and take you home from there?" Cheryl nodded quickly, afraid he might offer to take them himself. That could be dangerous.

They had Mama lie down on a stretcher and loaded her in the ambulance. Rosie, Kati and Kari rode up front and Cheryl stayed in the back with Mama. Mama was still screaming "bloody murder." The ambulance driver yelled back at Cheryl, "I need to radio into the hospital. What exactly do you think is wrong with your mother?"

Cheryl leaned over to Mama. "Mama, what should I tell him?" Bea stopped screaming for a moment and said, calmly, "Tell him I've had a nervous breakdown several times. It's probably another."

Mama resumed screaming again. Cheryl relayed the message and they sped toward the hospital. Once Mama was in the emergency room the girls settled in the waiting room. Cheryl found a phone and called the boys first, then the pastor of the church.

He arrived shortly and waited with the girls until the doctor came out to talk with them. "I think she'll be fine. She's just a little hysterical over the accident. We've given her a shot and she'll sleep the night. We'll keep her overnight for observation then release her tomorrow." The minister thanked the doctor, then he took the girls home. "I'll be back tomorrow to take you to pick her up. Are you sure you'll be all right by yourselves tonight?"

Cheryl assured him they would be, and he turned and left. Long after the other kids were asleep, Cheryl lay considering an idea that had come into her head during the wait at the hospital. It was a daring plan, but it just might work.

On the way to the hospital the next morning, Cheryl asked the pastor, "Will you do me a big favor? Mama will be real embarrassed at seeing you without her hair and makeup fixed, so will you have her ride in the back seat? Also, would you keep your head down and not look at her directly. She might get real upset again and start screaming if she feels like you're looking at her and thinking she looks bad."

The pastor smiled and shook his head. Patting Cheryl on the shoulder, he said, "Don't worry, Cheryl, I wouldn't want to say or do a thing that would upset your mama. Trust me. I won't raise an eyebrow at her," he chuckled.

That was phase one of Cheryl's plan. Now for phase two. "If you'll just wait in the car, I'll go in and help her out to the car." The pastor agreed to this also. Cheryl jumped out of the car and ran into the hospital. Mama was already sitting at the front desk, ready to go. Cheryl took a deep breath. It was now or never. Phase three.

"Mama, Rev. Sawyer is out in his car. He didn't want to come in. He's going to take you home, but he doesn't want you coming to church anymore."

Mama looked startled, "Why in the world not?" She was shocked.

"I told him, Mama. I told him everything," Cheryl began. She looked Mama squarely in the eye, forcing herself to maintain unwavering eye contact. It felt as if every cell in her body was vibrating with fear. Mama's eyes narrowed; it seemed she was staring a hole into Cheryl's soul. Cheryl sensed the heat flaring up in Mama's face and ears. Bea's nostrils were flaring and her breathing rate escalated. "What do you mean?" Bea's voice was low and even, defying her facial expression.

Cheryl kept her voice equally controlled. "I mean I told him everything. I told him that you force me to go to men and let them do things and they give you money. I told him that you beat every one of us kids to a bloody pulp on a regular basis. I told him that Daddy sells pornography and where he has a big stash of material. I told him Daddy has perverted pictures. I told him Daddy has broken our ribs and collar bones and cracked our skulls with his pounding fists. I told him that you and Daddy starve us sometimes and that you lock us up. I told him you treat us worse than the animals and sometimes make us eat off the floor like a dog and make us squeal like pigs. I told him we are always afraid and we don't want these things to happen anymore. I told him I want to save my little sisters from the humiliation, embarrassment and shame I've had to endure for years. I told him everything, Mama, I mean everything."

Mama was already popping nerve medicine (Valium). Her previously flushed face was now colorless. Beads of sweat were bursting out on her forehead. "Well," she said, trying to regain her composure, "he didn't believe you, did he?"

"Yes, Mama, he did believe me. Don't worry. He's not going to report you unless I report to him that it has happened again. Then he will report everything. He's willing to take you home now, but he doesn't want you to ever come back to his church. And, if we move away, he will report you immediately. He said they have ways of finding you. He doesn't even want to look at you. He wants you to ride in the back seat."

Cheryl felt enormous power because of the fear she could read in her mother's eyes. "Are you ready to go now?" she asked her mother.

Mama raised herself slowly from the wheelchair, and, head down, walked out to the car. She silently slid into the car then leaned her head back like she had immediately gone to sleep. The pastor had never even turned his head. He winked at Cheryl as she slid into the front seat beside him. She breathed a cautious sigh of relief. It had worked! It had WORKED! HALLELUJAH! IT HAD WORKED!!!

Now, maybe she could feel safe leaving the girls and could get out on her own. She'd have to test it for a little while to be sure, but it certainly appeared it had worked.

The next few weeks of their lives confirmed IT HAD WORKED! There was still abuse, still beatings, and though still severe, much less so and much less frequently. Finally some deliverance had come. Now maybe, finally she could feel the younger girls were safe enough that she could leave. Cheryl knew God had to have helped her with the master plan. It had gone so smoothly that there had to have been some divine intervention.

Cheryl felt very powerful and very much in control for the first time ever. The fear that registered in Bea's eyes when Cheryl told her that the pastor had believed her was an amazing bonus. For years Cheryl had been told that grownups never believe children. Bea just confirmed what she'd suspected all along but had not had the courage to test. Children and grownups alike will listen and believe when it is the truth. That was a valuable piece of information to know.

FOURTEEN

Martin had turned off the car radio, believing Cheryl to be asleep. The steady hum of the tires against the highway was a comforting sound as she drifted in and out of sleep. Martin was a really nice guy and, at the moment, he was her rescuer. Cheryl was leaving home at seventeen and she knew without a doubt that she would never again return.

The students at school made fun of Martin. He was rather odd, but Cheryl identified with him and had befriended him. Ironically, it was Martin who helped her escape her abusive home life. With his thick glasses, slicked-down hair, and an overweight body stuffed into Big Smith jeans and a flannel shirt, Martin did not fit in with other trendy teenagers.

Cheryl never fit in either. She was always the new student and never had anything new or stylish to wear. When her legs were not terribly bruised, she would attempt to fit in by hiking her skirt up or rolling it at the waist to shorten the length. Her hair was long again, and with money she earned babysitting other children occasionally, she could sometimes buy shampoo and keep it clean.

Both Cheryl and Martin were good students but social misfits in the senior class. The girls disliked Cheryl. She supposed it was because she didn't dress like them or socialize with them. However, the main reason was probably that the boys all crowded around her. The Morgan family always lived in smaller towns and most of the students had grown up together. In high school, when Cheryl would enter a new school all the boys were anxious to get to know "the new girl." Cheryl's "dates" were almost always limited to lunch dates in the school cafeteria because Renny and Bea severely restricted her social life.

Martin understood the restriction because his parents also limited his social life. He had an invalid mother, an alcoholic father, and a mentally impaired younger brother. Though each knew only a little about the other's burdens and responsibilities, Martin and Cheryl gravitated toward and guarded each other.

A few weeks earlier, midway through the third nine weeks of her senior year in high school, Cheryl ran away from home. She'd established a friendship with a girl who'd already graduated, and the girl helped her escape. After only a few days, Cheryl called home to check on her brothers and sisters. Bea told her that her youngest sister, Rosie, was very sick and crying for her. Cheryl had tried to stay indifferent but instead she caved in and returned home. She wished she could stay away long periods of time like Richie and Davey.

Returning home, she discovered that, not surprisingly, Renny and Bea had lied to her. Rosie was healthy and had actually not been sick at all. All the kids were delighted to have Cheryl back home. There were still two empty places at the table for Davey and Richie. There was a sense of stability, of balance and peace in the midst of the storm, when all seven of the children were together. Isolated from the others, they felt vulnerable and unprotected. Somehow just the presence of each other was comforting.

Bea was very incensed at Cheryl's streak of daring and inde pendence. During the few days that Cheryl had been gone, Bea had conjured up absurd punishments, "house rules" for Cheryl to follow.

As a "run-away" Cheryl was first stripped and beaten by Renny. At first they were going to require Cheryl to sleep in the garage with the German shepherd dog. Upon further deliberation they figured it would be easier for her to run away again if she slept in the garage. A flip-over lock was installed on the outside of a bedroom door where Cheryl was locked up every night. All the chores of the other children were suspended for them and del egated to Cheryl.

Though she prepared all the meals and did all the clean-up, she was not permitted to eat with the family. After everyone else had eaten she would be allowed to eat, without utensils, from the floor. If she chose to endure this humiliation in order to eat, Renny and Bea would force her to make oinking noises as she ate.

They would stand above her alternately kicking, name-calling, and shouting degrading remarks. None of the other children was allowed to either look at or speak to Cheryl directly. They did so with extreme caution and at great personal risk. Even at school they dared not risk much contact with her for fear that Renny or

Bea would be lurking around a corner. Cheryl had been taken to school and picked up to be returned immediately to her personal prison.

In those few days Cheryl had been gone, she'd discovered that it would be difficult to get a job without a high school diploma. Upon her return home Cheryl had been, in her parents' words, reduced to slave status and therefore had no rights, even to a bed or blanket. She was to sleep on the floor.

One amazing "right" that she was promised conditionally was to go to college. Her strong desire, or dream, was to attend college, and that desire was no secret to Bea. Bea agreed to a "bargain" with Cheryl. She would have to voluntarily remain in "slave status" for one year after high school graduation. In return for the one year of additional "service," Bea and Renny would ask Renny's parents to pay her way to college. Cheryl believed they would ask her grandparents to pay. She was willing to pay the price required. It never occurred to her they might never ask, or even that she could ask for herself.

Another punishment was that Cheryl was to be cut off socially from everyone including any school activities and church attendance. Being robbed of going to church was the most difficult punishment for Cheryl. It meant the few short hours of peace she experienced in a week were removed from her otherwise stormy existence.

On weekends Cheryl was to be locked in a bedroom except when doing specifically assigned chores for Renny or Bea. Bea felt she needed to break the independent nature of her oldest daughter and this was the only way to accomplish it. Cheryl had run away from home several times and never appeared to be remorseful except for being homesick for the other children. Bea saw herself as a good mother. She'd trained Cheryl to cook and sew and care for children. Cheryl would make a good wife for someone.

Bea had taught her daughter to be responsible and taught her about life. Cheryl seemed to have a fantasy that she was going to be somebody and do something with her life. Bea wanted to dash those hopes for Cheryl. It would shield her from disappointments in the future. Cheryl had to learn to expect nothing from others and take everything she could. Bea had once been a visionary herself, imagining herself becoming an artist or a famous singer. The reality she'd experienced in her life didn't even come close to the dreams she'd held onto. Now she was almost thirty-six years old and Cheryl was almost eighteen. Cheryl's life was probably going to end up the same way. She'd get married to a man who would promise her the world and deliver very little.

Cheryl would probably be as fertile as her mother and end up pregnant year after year. Bea did worry about that part a little bit. She had given "the pill" to Cheryl for so many years she was afraid it might cause problems for her. One of the brands of birth control pills she'd given Cheryl for over a year had even been pulled off the market because of dangerous side effects.

Well, pretty soon it wouldn't be her problem anyway. Cheryl probably would not make the connection to blame Bea for infertility. As far as Bea knew, Cheryl didn't know she'd been taking birth control for years. Bea decided not to think about it anymore. It was a practiced survival skill for her.

Another defect Bea saw in Cheryl was that she was a thinker and had a quick, alert mind. Bea didn't like it. Renny was a thinker too, a thinker of schemes and lies, deceptions and impossible dreams. Heavy thinkers and quick thinking people, in Bea's estimation, were also very good liars. Renny was a diagnosed paranoid schizophrenic and had an extremely high IQ. The prison psychiatrist said that he had a genius mentality. Renny was a part of the Menses society, and proud of it. Bea guessed that Cheryl probably had inherited her father's high IQ. She needed to break that free-thinking spirit in Cheryl. If she could cut her off from any creative input, it should squelch her imagination, hopes and dreams.

Bea knew what it was like to keep hoping in someone for years and years. It was like an addiction, an obsessive habit that was out of her control. In her mind Bea knew that life with Renny would always be the same, but her heart always judged him to be sincere. Bea believed Renny would always be involved with pornography, always be on the run and on the move. He would always speak of his newest "get rich quick" scheme with such confidence, such conviction, that she invariably believed him. Sometimes the lines between fact and fiction were so obscured that Renny himself wasn't sure of the real truth.

It seemed to Bea that Cheryl also was a good liar. Most of the time it was convenient for Bea and Renny to utilize this peculiar talent in Cheryl, but it had caused them some problems. Bea wasn't sure if there really had been a conversation between Cheryl and the preacher, but she had no way to verify it. She was going to have to break that lying in Cheryl too, except where truth would endanger herself, Renny or the children. Bea believed she really did have Cheryl's best interests at heart.

* * *

Riding with Martin in the car now, Cheryl couldn't imagine she'd survived weeks and weeks of the kind of treatment her parents had imposed with their "rules." Everyone has a breaking point, and this day Cheryl had reached hers.

Three nights previously she'd had her high school graduation in the football stadium. Martin had taken her. Bea said her back was bothering her and they probably would not attend. All through the graduation Cheryl had scanned the stands for her mother and father. She never did find their faces. As she stepped across the platform to receive her diploma, she saw Martin approaching the stairs she would descend.

Flushed and excited, Martin was swallowed up in a mass bouquet of seventy-two blue and white carnations (the school colors). The year was 1972 and the flowers were the most exciting gift Martin could think of for Cheryl. Though everyone laughed and Cheryl was extremely embarrassed, inwardly she was pleased at Martin's gesture of devotion.

Martin drove Cheryl home to check in with Renny and Bea. "Why didn't you come to my graduation?" Cheryl asked, trying not to cry or show her disappointment. They explained that they had gone to the graduation, but left as soon as Cheryl had received her diploma.

Bea looked up from her crocheting and said, "My back is bad, and I can't sit in those stadium seats. You understand, don't you?" Not really, thought Cheryl. If it were my kid I wouldn't care if I had to be carried in on a stretcher, I'd be there. Martin's mother had come in a wheelchair. Out loud, Cheryl replied, "Yes, Mama." Now was a good time to ask if she could go to Martin's house for a little celebration. She was still restricted to the house rules. It was almost surprising they had let her go to her high school graduation. Renny and Bea talked a little then agreed to let her go to Martin's for one hour.

Martin's mother had gotten a cake at the bakery that said, "Congratulations Martin and Cheryl." It was the first time Cheryl had eaten a bakery cake and the first time she'd had one decorated for her. She was very moved by Martin's mother for including her in their family celebration. She never told Renny and Bea about the carnations. Thanking Martin profusely, she left them at his house for his mother to enjoy. After the one-hour allotted celebration was over, Martin took her back home and dropped her at the door.

When Cheryl opened the front door, Bea was standing behind it and jumped out in back of her. Whirling around, Cheryl was startled, not knowing what to expect. Bea handed her an envelope. Cheryl was too stunned to say anything. "Well, open it," Bea demanded, smiling. "It's your graduation present from Daddy and me."

Cheryl tore open the envelope and read the hand-made card. Inside it said, "This card is good for one dinner out and a movie, tomorrow night." She couldn't believe it. After weeks of strict confinement, put-downs, sub-human treatment, here was a gift, and a smile. It was also going to be her first movie in a theatre. She had seen one movie, "A Raisin' in the Sun," shown in the school gymnasium when she was in about fifth or sixth grade. Mama had said back then that moviegoers would all go to hell.

Cheryl had sat with her three brothers in the gym, all four of them shaking and terrified that God was going to catch them watching the movie and come throw them into "the lake of fire" in hell. They had survived, however, and Mama had changed her beliefs, partially because of the television, partially because she'd mellowed with time.

This was unbelievable that she would go to a movie with Daddy and Mama and also get to go out to eat. Mama snatched the envelope out of her hand and sat back down. "We'll go tomorrow night. Get to the bedroom now so Daddy can lock you in for the night."

As Renny was pulling the door shut, Cheryl leaned out the doorway, "Thank you, Daddy. Thank you, Mama. It's a really nice present." It seemed too good to be true that they had come through with the gift. The next night all three went out to eat and then to the movie of Cheryl's choice, "The Andromeda Strain." It was an intense science fiction movie and Cheryl was caught away every moment of the entire film. After the movie she was locked away again in the bedroom.

Cheryl had been asleep for a while when she was awakened as the door burst open. Renny snatched her from the floor and thrust her through the open door. Half standing, half crawling, she made it to the living room. She tried to shake herself awake and alert amid Renny and Bea's yelling. Renny roughly pulled Cheryl's wrists together behind her back and tied them. Bea was directly in front of her. Cheryl was five feet seven inches tall, about five inches taller than her mother. Reaching up, Bea slapped her hard across the face. "Are you smoking pot?" she screamed. It was more of a statement than an accusation.

Cheryl was astounded by the question. She'd never even smoked a regular cigarette. "No, Mama, I've never smoked pot. Really! It's the truth."

Bea slapped her again on the other cheek. Renny pushed a chair up behind Cheryl, forcing her to sit down. "That's better," Bea said, thrusting her chin out. It was Renny's theory that the more he towered over a person, the more superior it made him. On the flip side it would make his "victim" feel much more inadequate and inferior. Bea too found it to be very effective. Again Bea screamed, "You've been smoking pot, haven't you?" as her hand again descended on Cheryl's face. Again Cheryl intensely denied the charges.

"It smells like this," Renny said. He suspended a thick rope above Cheryl's head. Lighting it he lowered it and swung the burning rope like a pendulum at eye level, close to her face. She could smell the burning rope, feel the heat and hear the crackling of her own hair being singed by the flickering flames and sparks.

Repeatedly, Renny and Bea accused her of smoking marijuana. Again and again Cheryl emphatically and defiantly denied it. It was the truth and she resolved to stand by the truth. She didn't know how much time had passed when she crumbled under their interrogation. Her face and neck felt huge and swollen. She could feel the heat radiating from her numb face. Her head was pounding from the repeated blows, the smoldering rope smell, and the heat.

She felt nauseated from the blood she had swallowed from

her bloodied lips and nose. Her lips were so distended from the injuries inflicted that she couldn't close her mouth. The heat, pain, nausea, facial numbness, and ringing, driving pain in her ears all combined to disintegrate her resolve. It was hopeless. Bea was not going to give up or tire until she got the answer she wanted. Cheryl painfully forced herself to form the words, "I admit it. I've smoked pot."

"It's about time," said Bea triumphantly. "I knew we would break you. Go to the bathroom and wash your face. Daddy's going to lock you in your room for twenty-four hours, and then we'll let you out and see what you have to say for yourself."

Cheryl had wearily dragged herself to the bathroom, splashed some cool water on her face and eased down to the floor in the bedroom. She was glad to hear the lock flip over on the outside of the door.

Bright sunlight was pouring in through a tear in the window blind, spilling across her face. Cheryl rose up and felt a throbbing, splitting ache in her head. She painfully crawled over to the window and raised herself up on her elbows. Peering carefully through the side of the pulled-down blind, Cheryl's heart jumped when she saw that Renny and Bea's cars were both gone. She tiptoed over to the bedroom door and listened carefully.

Saturday morning cartoons could be heard on the television and the girls were arguing. She didn't hear Eddie's voice. That was good, too. Lately Eddie was such a snitch, doing whatever it took to make himself look good. Cautiously she lightly knocked on the door. After a few times she finally heard Kari outside.

"Kari, honey, please open the door. I have to go to the bathroom."

"Mama and Daddy said I can't let you out. I'll be in big trouble."

"Kari," Cheryl wondered why she was still whispering, "where are they?"

"Mama went to get her hair fixed and Daddy went to the flea market," Kari whispered back.

"Kari, you know they let me out to go to the bathroom. Please open the door."

"Okay." Cheryl could hear her fumbling with the flip-over lock. She opened the door. "Cheryl, what happened to you?" Kari threw her arms around her and started to cry. Cheryl held her a few moments then unwillingly pushed her away. She knew her time was short.

"Kari, where is Eddie?"

"He went with Daddy to the flea market."

"Did they say when they'd be back?"

"No, they just said for me to fix some sandwiches for Kati and Rosie if they weren't back by lunch," Kari answered.

By now the other two girls were in the hallway. They all cried when they saw their sister's bruised, swollen, and badly distorted face. "Girls, I have to hurry. I have to run away again. I promise, someday I'll come back for you, but I just can't stay. I can't." Cheryl headed down the hallway to the kitchen phone. She dialed Martin's number, praying he would be home. Thankfully he answered.

"Martin, this is Cheryl. I'm in trouble. Mama and Daddy nearly killed me last night. You've got to come help me get away.

I have to leave NOW. They're gone now, but I don't know for how long. If I don't get away now, I don't think I'll ever get away." Cheryl was crying now and the other girls were clinging to her and crying, too.

"I'm out the door. I'll be right there," Martin said, and the line went dead.

Cheryl knew he would be there in about ten minutes. There wasn't much time to get anything. The most important matter was to have a heart-to-heart with the little girls. Kati was twelve, Kari ten, and Rosie was five. She warned them, "Don't ever end up alone in the house with Daddy. If he calls you aside, try to take someone with you. Don't let Mama and Daddy force you to do anything that hurts your insides."

"How can we do that?" Kati asked. It was a realistic question. Cheryl didn't have power over Renny or Bea, and she was much older, wiser, and stronger than the little girls. She desperately wished she could take them with her.

"I don't know, but I have to warn you. Just try to be careful. It's a lie that the law won't do anything. Mama is scared of the preacher at our old church. With her you can say that Cheryl told you to call that preacher collect. She'll get really mad and will probably beat you, but she won't let Daddy have ex-con buddies come in and touch you in a bad way."

Cheryl couldn't risk telling them of her deception with Mama. They probably couldn't understand anyway. She wished she could cram years of her own experience into them in a few moments. The best she could do was to promise to visit them and most of all to pray for them.

The most difficult part was now. "I'm never coming back home to live, but I will come and visit you at your schools. I'll find ways to see you. I'll come back for you. I promise. When you get lonely for me, sing our song. I bet I'll be singing it too, wherever I am."

Their song was the chorus of "Love Lifted Me." They gathered in a tight circle, arms entangled, getting as close to each other as possible and sang together, "Love lifted me, love lifted me, when nothing else could help, love lifted me." Cheryl hugged and kissed all three over and over. Breaking loose, she ran into the bedroom and grabbed up three shirts, two pairs of jeans, a sweater, a few family pictures and her purse. Kati ran to get a paper sack while the other girls watched for Martin's car.

"Sometimes I hate Mama and Daddy," Kari said, hugging her sister tight around the waist.

"Sometimes I do too, Kari, but it's wrong. But, I want you to know that what they're doing to us is wrong, too. Someday it's going to stop." Cheryl said.

"I wish they'd both just die. When Daddy's gone lots of times I pray that he'll never come back, or that he'll get killed in a car wreck, or that one of his prison friends will get mad at him and have the mafia kill him. Sometimes I wish that on Mama too, but I hate Daddy more," Kari confessed.

Martin pulled up in front of the house. Cheryl peeled her crying sisters away from her. "I love you, Kati! I love you, Kari! And I love you Rosie!" She kissed and hugged them all again. "I'll always be able to find you through Grandma and Grandpa. Don't worry, I'll be safe and I'll come back and visit you. Someday, I'll take you with me."

Before she changed her mind or ran out of time, she jumped into Martin's car and sped away. They went to his house where she showered and changed. Martin's mother doctored Cheryl's face and gave her a cool compress to put on it. His mother wanted them to stay, but Cheryl knew Martin's was the first place Renny would look for her.

"I have to get out of state. Daddy will find me here. I have to get far away, but close enough to come visit the girls."

After some discussion it was decided that Martin and his brother would go and take Cheryl to Oklahoma City or Tulsa, Oklahoma. Martin had relatives in Oklahoma City and friends in Tulsa where Cheryl could stay until she got a job. With that decision made, Martin's mother had pressed a twenty-dollar bill into Cheryl's hand, more money into Martin's hand. They loaded up and took off for Oklahoma. Since Tulsa was further away, it ended up being Cheryl's choice destination, a five-hour drive.

Her mother had broken Cheryl's resolve to maintain her stance on the truth about the marijuana, but she had not broken her spirit.

Cheryl was going to show them that she could make it despite the destruction levied on her over the past seventeen years. So, just weeks before her 18th birthday, Cheryl arrived in Tulsa. A five-foot-seven, eighty-pound frail frame offered a sharp contrast to the real Cheryl, a strong-willed survivor. She hadn't survived seventeen years of abuse to be defeated by the world.

By the end of the summer Cheryl had rented her own tiny one-room efficiency apartment in downtown Tulsa. It had a bathroom, a "Murphy bed," and a closet converted into a kitchenette. She made a few friends, learned some new grooming habits, and bought a few articles of clothing. After working in a fast food restaurant a few days, Cheryl was determined to get out of food service. She risked lying about her age, skills and experience, and luckily landed a job as a legal secretary making $350 per month.

It was only a temporary position, open for six months while the attorney's permanent secretary was on maternity leave. The attorney was a criminal lawyer and had very little office work for her to do. She answered the phone and read and summarized court reporters' notes. During that six months Cheryl taught herself office skills in the one-person office. She lived very frugally on cinnamon toast, macaroni and cheese, peanut butter and Wheaties.

The first three weeks of her employment she wore the same little red sailor dress every day. A lady in the office down the hall noticed and one day brought in a sack of dresses for Cheryl to have. She was overcome by this stranger's kindness. By the time the secretarial job ended, she'd paid her rent for an extra two months and had saved enough to take two classes at the local junior college.

The legal secretary job ended mid-January, which was also when college classes began. Cheryl was delighted she could take the two classes. She had no concept what a "credit hour" was or how long it would take for her to graduate at the rate of six credit hours per semester. A perceptive guidance counselor observed Cheryl struggling with registration forms. He pulled up a chair and assisted her. Thanking him, she turned to leave, but he ran after her. "Do you have a job?"

"Well, as of today, no. But, I'll find one soon I'm sure." She turned to go again.

"Wait, I'm Mr. Barnes. I noticed on your application that you've been doing secretarial work."

"That's right."

"Well, it just so happens I need a secretary. I'm the guidance counselor for evening students. Could you work 5pm to 9pm?"

"I don't know. I need to work full time. Didn't you notice my classes are both night classes? I'm totally self-supporting," Cheryl informed him.

"Are your parents deceased?"

Cheryl hesitated, "No, they've disowned me."

"That could be beneficial to you." Mr. Barnes was smiling. "Why don't you come back and see me in my office at five o'clock. I'll interview you for the job and we'll talk some more. I'll show you where to find me." Mr. Barnes seemed nice enough, but Cheryl remained cautious.

She went back that evening and talked at length with Mr. Barnes. He was a very nice man, a Baptist, in fact, and he had grown children. Cheryl had a special love for the Baptists. They were usually the ones with good bus ministries interested in poor children. He was a diabetic and told her he had marks on his stomach and thighs from all the needles he had to puncture his body with every day.

Cheryl had never known a diabetic and listened with great interest as he told her all about his medical history. Finally he had gotten down to the bottom line with Cheryl. "Why are you here in Tulsa, and why are you on your own?"

Cheryl didn't divulge too much but enough to let him know

she was needy. "Would your parents sign a paper stating that they've disowned you?"

Cheryl panicked and rose to leave. She wasn't about to let Renny and Bea know where she was. She called Grandma and Grandpa Morgan periodically and let them know she was all right, but she didn't trust anyone with where she was. She had hitch-hiked back to Texas to visit the girls a few times, but even they didn't know where she was living.

Martin, his brother and mother were the only people that knew where she was, and she didn't even trust them with her address. After almost eight months she still woke up screaming in the night with nightmares that Renny and Bea had found her and were coming to take her back into the hell she'd finally escaped.

Mr. Barnes read the terror in her eyes. "Sit back down, Cheryl. We won't contact them. Nobody's going to hurt you here. I think with all the information you've given me so far, I can get some grants and loans that would allow you to go to school full time. Would you like that?"

It seemed an impossible dream was about to come true. "But how? I don't have money... I don't have a job..."

"You've got a job – working for me if you want it. That will give you money to live on – about $65 every two weeks. I can get you loans and grants for your tuition, books and housing. Are you interested?"

"Yes, sir!" Cheryl couldn't hide her elation. With the help of Mr. Barnes, Cheryl's financial needs and educational needs were taken care of. This would allow her time to concentrate on healing in the emotional and spiritual areas of her life. It was going to be a long journey, but a successful one, to be victorious over the abuse she had endured.

FIFTEEN

L iving alone was an adjustment for Cheryl. Up until now she'd never had any real time to think or meditate. Waking hours had always been too laden with simple survival. There was a gnawing concern about the anger and fear she felt.

When she was awake, she knew that she was safe. Renny and Bea did not know where she lived. There was a good lock on her door. At eighteen years old she was now "legal" and believed they could not force her to return home, even if they did find her. A remark about "legal age" overhead in the cafeteria disturbed the slight peace turning eighteen had given her. That conversation had indicated that a person was not considered a legal adult until the age of twenty-one. That few minutes of eavesdropping induced three more years of anxiety and nightmares for Cheryl.

She had very few friends, keeping a distance for "security purposes." Another lost soul, Lily, a Finnish young woman who barely spoke English, became a good friend. Cheryl helped Lily with classes that required good language skills. Lily helped Cheryl with technical classes: algebra, geography and physical sciences. Sometimes she would bring food for them to share at lunch. The girls complemented each other academically and helped each other adjust to college life.

It was difficult for her to relate to many other students. Even being away from Renny and Bea's restrictions and abuses, she was still held prisoner by the memories. No matter what she did, nothing was going to change what had happened during her lifetime. She desperately wanted to tell somebody what had been done to her. There never seemed to be anyone worthy of that much trust.

She detected something in their eyes, their words, that would convince her that no one would believe her anyway. Even if they did believe her, they'd look at her differently, knowingly. It would be worse than keeping the dark secrets of her past. What would be the use of telling anyway? Nothing could be done about it now. It could be dangerous for the rest of the kids still at home. Besides, no one could restore anything that had already been taken from her. Could anyone give back a clear mind, untainted memories, and innocence? How about trust, pure love, self-respect?

Her tiny apartment seemed to be an incubator for the worst memories. There was no television or radio, but her mind played scenes deep into the night hours.

At 9:05pm, Monday through Friday, Mr. Barnes always dropped her at the door of the building, even though it was only two blocks away from the school. He said that a young lady shouldn't be out alone in downtown Tulsa after dark. How little he knew! Cheryl found nothing to fear in the physical darkness of the night.

After the first year of junior college, Mr. Barnes transferred to another city and a better job. Cheryl panicked, but he assured her that his replacement, Mr. Larson, would be just as kind to her and as unquestioning and protective as he had been. Thankfully, Mr. Larson was a wonderful man who favored and watched over Cheryl, just as Mr. Barnes had promised.

Cheryl found the weekends were very long. At first she spent most of the time holed up in the apartment. Very soon she discovered that too much time alone in the apartment began to erode her resolve to never return home. She would begin thinking about the girls and worrying about them, feeling she needed to go back for their protection. Getting an education, a good job, and making it on her own were the best defenses she could offer the girls. If they saw her leave and make it, she knew they'd follow in her footsteps. Dating was a means of escape for Cheryl as well as a free meal ticket for cuisine finer than she had ever experienced. Dating also offered a wide variety of entertainment that was all new to her. She was taken to movies, football games, basketball games, ballets, rock concerts and parties.

Sensing power in making her own decisions, power over her circumstances, and power over whomever she wanted in her life were also great new feelings. Cheryl had made a few very important decisions. The first decision was that she would never again attend church. God hadn't rescued her from her circumstances; she'd had to escape on her own.

Church people had let Mama and Daddy attend church and never detected how vicious, evil and mean they were to their children. It seemed to Cheryl that if church people were so good, they surely should have been able to discern how deceitful and false her parents were. The Bible said that good and evil couldn't associate; yet church people had associated with Mama and Daddy.

They had to have been at least slightly suspicious of all the wounds, bruises and broken bones the children were always experiencing. Yet, not one person had ever taken steps to get to the truth. They turned their heads the other way. Pointing and whispering behind Mama and Daddy's backs, the fine, upstanding church people were friendly to their faces. Smiling and chatting, laughing at Renny's moronic joking, they avoided looking directly at the children. Some even shunned the Morgan children who were never quite clean enough or dressed well enough to be worthy of touching.

Of course she had to remember that there were also many church people who had been very kind, gentle and loving to the Morgan children, especially the churches Renny and Bea had never attended. Sunday school teachers and bus ministry people in particular had always made sure the children felt loved and welcomed.

Cheryl had spent many Sunday mornings squeezed up tight in the pew against a much-admired Sunday school teacher. She'd waited patiently in line getting on and off the bus with the other children. Not for the candy or other treat being offered, but for a pat on the shoulder, a gentle ruffling of her hair, a quick hug from one of the workers. One of her favorite memories was cat napping on the bus or in a pew next to her Sunday school teachers. One of the littler kids would be on Cheryl's lap (usually Rosie or Kari), and another (usually Kati or Richie) would be in the lap of the teacher. It was a secure, carefree and safe feeling. Now that Cheryl had decided to stay away from church forever, she had to squelch those memories. That was a skill at which she was well practiced, so it was not a difficult challenge.

In college dating she found the guys were delighted with her excitement and enthusiasm with whatever activity they chose for the evening. The poor lads had no idea that most activities were new experiences for her. The only way she knew to repay them was in casual sex. She didn't really consider it a sin; after all, she was already ruined anyway, what was the difference? It was rather pleasant to have that kind of power over her own body. No one asked her to do anything perverted, and she was always in control of what did or did not transpire. That power of decision over her own body offered a wonderful sense of freedom. Finally, there were no bruises to hide or be ashamed of either.

Over the years she, as well as her brothers and sisters, had learned to numb their emotions. It was a form of self-preservation. Control over revealing or concealing expressions of pain, sorrow, grief, pleasure, happiness, sadness or anger were the only defenses they were not stripped of by their parents. After a few months of being removed from the situation, Cheryl could see that really Renny and Bea were so very angry and frustrated with each other, not their children. It seemed they had vented their resentment, displeasure and hostility for each other onto their children. Other times it appeared they were allies with each other in a war in which the children were the enemy. One valid observation Cheryl made was that they were undeniably better at raising dogs than children.

Cheryl knew it was bizarre, but somehow she missed her mother and father. She was furious with herself for feeling that way. She knew she didn't want to go back. She knew it would be worse than ever before. Really and truly she was much happier and better off than she'd ever been. They must have made her crazy after all. How can a person love someone who nearly destroys his or her life? Her feelings of hatred toward Renny and Bea were just as intense as feelings of love for them. It was an awful conflict of heart issues.

Cheryl found another love to consume her life, her time, and her emotions – music. Signing up for a class, she fulfilled a lifetime dream of taking piano lessons. There was a problem with that, but the price to pay was small. The junior college had no facilities for piano instruction, so classes were given off campus. The only teacher within walking distance for Cheryl gave her lessons at a big downtown church. That meant she had to back off her vow to never again darken the door of a church. Exhausting every other choice on the list of instructors, Cheryl was forced to take lessons from the "church teacher."

God had been "bothering" Cheryl lately. It seemed He called to her in the night hours. She would shout out into the darkness, "Go away! Leave me alone! I don't believe in You anymore!" In an act of defiance, she took up cigarette smoking. When that failed to relieve the tension and sleepless nights, she found drugs could help ease the inner raging. Cheryl knew about penitentiaries and how the world looked at ex-cons. That knowledge kept her away from all illegal drugs except marijuana – and that was only rarely done under peer pressure at a party now and then (That one concession was in defiance to Bea, who'd wrongly accused her of it already). She learned she could go to different doctors for the same complaint and get legal drugs. They kept her well supplied with Valium, codeine, sleeping pills, and Percodan. This too presented a problem for Cheryl. It was exasperating to her that she still had a deep respect for the sacredness of a church sanctuary (God's House). She knew she'd be overwhelmed with guilt the minute she set foot inside.

However, the desire to play the piano triumphed over fear and guilt, and she marched in to her first lesson. Mrs. Selvey liked Cheryl immediately because she was such an eager student and quick learner. She obtained special permission from the church for Cheryl to come practice whenever she wanted in a Sunday school room upstairs. Every spare moment she could find, Cheryl was at the keyboard. At the end of her first nine weeks she played for "jury," a board of music teachers who gave a mid-term grade based on one performance of one piece of music.

Cheryl selected "Jesu, Joy of Man's Desiring" and played it flawlessly. Mrs. Selvey was very pleased and took Cheryl out to eat. It was the beginning of a wonderful friendship. Little by little she taught Cheryl some additional grooming. Cheryl had become a little "flower child," wearing only jeans, t-shirts or smock tops, sandals and long, straight hair, parted down the middle. Mrs. Selvey got her to add a few more feminine touches like earrings and cologne. In reality she was much more concerned about Cheryl's spiritual condition.

Cheryl knew that Mrs. Selvey knew she took (legal) drugs

and smoked cigarettes and that she partied. Amazingly, Mrs. Selvey never condemned her; neither did she condone the behavior. She always invited her to church, but Cheryl never came. One day, however, Mrs. Selvey gave Cheryl an offer she couldn't refuse. Another girl had moved in with Cheryl and was heavily into illegal drugs. It made Cheryl extremely nervous, and she confided her fears to Mrs. Selvey. The next piano lesson Mrs. Selvey startled Cheryl with an astonishing offer. Mr. Selvey had given his approval for Mrs. Selvey to rent a bedroom in their home to her. Cheryl was ecstatic. There were, however, Mrs. Selvey warned, some "house rules" that she would have to follow.

Cheryl steeled herself for what she would have to endure. She breathed an immense sigh of relief as Mrs. Selvey handed her a list. The listed included: no taking prescription drugs, no smoking in the house, help with household chores, practice piano daily, and attend church every Sunday. That would be a breeze. Church would be a little hurdle, but secretly she'd had a desire to attend anyway. This was a respectable way out of her vow to never go again.

Mrs. Selvey didn't know Cheryl had ever been to church. Cheryl was too ashamed to let her know that she knew better than to take pills and smoke and live the lifestyle she did. She figured it'd be good for Mrs. Selvey to think she'd taken in a little heathen child that she could reform. Cheryl knew it was deceptive, but it seemed justifiable and harmless.

The few months Cheryl lived with Mr. and Mrs. Selvey, she became much more "respectable" (in her own eyes). She met and became engaged to a young man named Patrick. He had a wonderful father and mother and two older sisters that were married and had children. An older brother had been killed in a car accident while attending college. A huge portrait of him hung prominently in the living room.

They had magnificent family gatherings with all the family for Sunday dinners, family celebrations and holidays. It was like being in a T.V. family. Mealtimes were delightful experiences where everyone laughed, talked loud, loved, and praised each other. Cheryl felt she was fulfilling her destiny. She would marry into this wonderful family, have many children and raise them in this incredible, loving family circle.

About the time Cheryl became engaged, Mr. Larson, Cheryl's boss at the junior college, got a new assistant named Carla. Carla was older than Cheryl and "world-wise." She was the only child of doting parents and had been given nearly everything her heart desired. Carla was in love with Mr. Larson, and Cheryl was her only confidant. Other people wouldn't understand, Carla confided in Cheryl. Mr. Larson was much older than Carla and both of them were recently divorced. Carla said it just wouldn't look good for Mr. Larson's job or hers if anyone knew. Cheryl appreciated Carla's trusting her.

One weekend Carla invited her to stay at her house. Mr. Larson came over and they all three had dinner together. Later that night she decided to test Carla and confide a tiny bit of information about herself to her. After that night Carla and Cheryl didn't talk about their shared secrets anymore. They did talk about many other things, though. They talked about dreams and discussed their beliefs and superstitions. With each other's help they listed life goals and impossible aspirations. It was Carla that convinced Cheryl she needed to take an aptitude test through the college to find out what talents and skills she really had.

Carla made Cheryl question whether she really wanted her life to be that of simply being a housewife and the mother of Patrick's children. The aptitude tests confirmed that Cheryl really did have intellectual abilities that could enable her to achieve some goals she formerly had considered unattainable.

It was with great sadness that Cheryl realized it was not Patrick that she loved at all, but it was his family circle. Patrick was grieved when Cheryl called off their marriage three days before the wedding. Patrick's grandmother had made her a beautiful gown with hundreds of hand-sewn pearls. His parents had arranged for a lovely church wedding.

Patrick had already rented a one-bedroom apartment for them. His enormous family had given several showers that filled a tiny apartment with everything they needed to establish a home. As desperately as she wanted a warm, loving family, a settledness with a home, husband, and children, Cheryl knew it wouldn't be enough. She had some deep issues to resolve before she could truly love anyone. Nearly everyone that knew Cheryl felt she was a fool for abandoning Patrick. That is, everyone except Mr. Larson and Carla.

Mr. Larson said, "You'll never be sorry for not marrying someone you don't love. Marrying just because everyone expects you to would put you both through a lifetime of hell on earth. I know, because that's the mistake I made." God knew Cheryl had already experienced enough hell on earth. She certainly was not going to voluntarily experience more.

Another one of Cheryl's supportive friends was Jane. Jane was another piano student of Mrs. Selvey, and she encouraged their friendship. It was with Jane that Cheryl got to experience some of the joys of being a teenager. Cheryl and Jane rode up and down "the strip" on Friday nights, yelled and waved at friends, drank wine coolers, and had "sleep-over's."

Since Cheryl had already moved out of the Selvey's home in anticipation of the wedding, she opted to go back to her own apartment. Now she had a friend who lived close by, and that friend had a car. It made it much easier to get around. Cheryl and Jane began to attend church together at the church where they took piano lessons. Cheryl began a journey of discovery into the spiritual wholeness that eventually would produce wholeness in every area of her life.

Together Jane and Cheryl gave up all their vices, except cigarettes. Cheryl settled back into the basic religious beliefs that had been instilled in her from the time she was a tiny child. Once again she began to experience the love and acceptance of genuine "church people."

Lacking one semester of finishing school at the junior college level, Cheryl applied for and was hired in a full-time secretarial position at a local university. She took the position in anticipation of establishing tuition benefits.

Evening classes at the junior college including music courses filled her evenings, until she met Leonard. Jane introduced them at church, and they liked each other immediately. That same night a group went out to eat. Afterward Leonard and Cheryl had paired off. Leonard went by "Leo," and from that day forward Leo and Cheryl were together every evening and every weekend.

Jane and Cheryl had sworn to each other that they would stay chaste until they married their husbands. Leo pressed Cheryl, but she stayed committed to the vow she'd made in church with Jane. Finally, after one month, Leo asked Cheryl to marry him. They had to wait a while until his divorce became final. Cheryl had some serious concerns about Leo but felt it might be her last chance to get married. She'd left Patrick practically at the altar less than a year earlier. She couldn't risk turning down a second proposal. She was already almost twenty-one years old. If she didn't marry Leo, she might never get married. Since she was going to marry him in a few weeks anyway, they moved in the same apartment building.

Not wanting to disappoint Jane, Mrs. Selvey or Mr. Larson and Carla (who were now married), Cheryl maintained her own efficiency apartment and Leo rented the apartment next door.

The wedding was scheduled to take place during Thanksgiving break. It was to be just a few months after Cheryl's 21st birthday. Turning twenty-one and on the verge of getting married, Cheryl felt it was safe to let her family know exactly where she was. She contacted her grandparents, who promised to try to get in touch with Renny and Bea. By now Renny and Bea had somehow purchased a large travel trailer. With the three girls they had been traveling around the country, living in the travel trailer. They went from city to city, state to state, selling merchandise at flea markets to make a living. Cheryl was sure Renny was probably still running some of his little side businesses.

Hank and Anna did manage to contact their wayward son a few days before the wedding. They called Cheryl and told her Renny, Bea and the girls would be there for the wedding. Not knowing if they would show up or not, Cheryl had Mr. Larson prepared to stand in to give her away. She wished the girls could be her bridesmaids, but it was too much pressure for her to handle the "iffy-ness" of the situation.

There was no telling what Renny and Bea had brainwashed the girls into thinking about her by now. She wasn't even sure if they would be there. She'd had Grandma Morgan tell them the colors of her wedding and instructed that the girls could handle the guest book, candle lighting for the wedding, and serving at the reception. Those were spots she had stand-ins for in case they didn't show.

Halfway through the wedding rehearsal there was a big commotion at the back of the church. Leo and Cheryl spun around and saw Rosie, Kari and Kati coming up the aisle, followed by Renny and Bea. Cheryl ran to the girls, scooping them into her arms, hugging and kissing them in a joyous reunion. Renny and Bea stood back, smiling convincingly. Cheryl nodded to them and then the rehearsal went on.

That night she slept on the floor of her tiny apartment with Rosie, Kari and Kati nestled close. Renny and Bea rented a motel room close by. She felt sure there would be no opportunity for a confrontation with all the people surrounding her for the wedding. Renny and Bea had always been careful to present a good public image. Cheryl's wedding was no exception.

The morning of the wedding she let the older girls try on the wedding gown. Kari especially was delighted with Cheryl's little apartment, even the "Murphy" bed. Adoringly, she said, "Cheryl, I want to be just like you when I grow up. I'll get an apartment just like this, go to college, and then get married… in your dress." The dress was borrowed, but Cheryl didn't bother to tell her.

A truce called in their life-long war with each other, Renny and Cheryl walked down the aisle together. Sweeping past a weeping Bea, who was radiant in a full length, white, flowing evening gown glittering with a rhinestone belt, Cheryl decided not to be irritated. She was sure that on down the line she'd be glad she had let them be part of her wedding day. Her life would continue successfully without them now, and she was permanently out of their reach.

After a honeymoon trip to Arizona and Texas, Leo and Cheryl both worked two jobs and purchased a modest home within the first year of their marriage. Cheryl never confided much to Leo about her life growing up. She did have to explain some things about her family's idiosyncrasies.

Leo had a large family circle in Texas and every holiday was spent with them. No decision in their marriage was made without Leo first consulting his mother. Cheryl resented what she considered to be a breach of the husband/wife relationship. She stifled those feelings, though, and convinced herself that she was glad to submit to him and become anything he wanted her to be.

His thoughts, his beliefs, his desires, his likes and dislikes became hers. Whatever he wanted to be or do, that's what she wanted. So desirous was she of a peaceful home, Cheryl dared not cross him in any area. Whatever the cost, she wanted a home that was strife-free. She cut off from all of her friends, including Mr. Larson, Carla, Lily and Jane. Leo's few friends became her only friends. It felt as if her feelings and opinions had no value. Her dreams and hopes for the future had to be laid aside for what Leo wanted. Cheryl felt like an empty shell, a non-person.

They attended church service on Sunday mornings and that was the extent of their spiritual involvement. Leo was uncomfortable saying grace at the table and even more uncomfortable if Cheryl got out a Bible. If keeping peace with Leo meant giving up God, it was a price she was willing to pay.

Cheryl got her associate's degree from the junior college then quit to help Leo with his studies to become an engineer. She even gave up piano. Leo was very jealous of her time and preferred her sitting next to him while he watched sports on television. Though he did purchase an old upright piano for her the first year they were married, he disliked the classical music she had been trained to play. Soon she gave up playing the piano, too.

With everything she cared about removed from her life, Cheryl began to experience "baby fever." Surprisingly, Leo gave his permission for her to discontinue birth control. Cheryl was amazed because Leo was in the process of giving up custody of a six-year-old son from his previous marriage to avoid paying child support of $60 per month. After two years of marriage Cheryl became pregnant. She was very excited and called Leo at work to tell him. He was very quiet on the other end of the phone. When she pressed him for a response, he simply said, "That's nice. I'm glad for you." Cheryl was very upset at his lack of excitement, but attributed it to shock that it had finally happened.

Later that week they had dinner with his secretary, Gwen. She was a single parent with a ten-year-old daughter and a six-year-old son. Cheryl had initially been pleased when Leo began helping Gwen with her yard, her car, and minor household repairs. She thought it was really sweet. Lately, though, it had begun to annoy her that Leo was so concerned about Gwen and her problems.

At dinner Gwen said, "Well, Cheryl, Leo tells me you're pregnant. I was really sorry to hear that. You're so young and you guys really haven't been married that long." It made Cheryl angry. What business was it of hers anyway? Cheryl was twenty-three years old now, and Leo was several years older than her. It was ridiculous for Gwen to say they were too young. Cheryl looked to Leo to make a statement of support, but he just pressed his lips together and with raised eyebrow, nodded his agreement with Gwen. Cheryl despised him at that moment for robbing her of the joy of the new life conceived within her.

It was a difficult pregnancy and Cheryl had morning sickness and nausea every night for the first few months. Leo would help her dress and insist she go to work. He didn't want any sickly little wife on his hands. His previous wife had pulled that stunt of morning sickness and quit her job mid-way through the pregnancy. Leo told Cheryl he would not permit her to quit her job.

The bigger Cheryl got, the later Leo stayed out at night. He began coming home later and later. At first he'd be home from work between 8 and 9pm, but soon it became 2 and 3am. He had obviously been drinking. One weekend he didn't come home at all. Cheryl drove around looking for him at the neighborhood bars. With a pounding heart she drove to where she had long suspected he might be. Sure enough, she found his car parked in front of Gwen's house. When he finally came home, Cheryl confronted him. Leo grabbed a suitcase and angrily packed it and moved in with Gwen. It was a little over a month before Cheryl's due date. Leo informed Cheryl that he didn't love her anymore; he loved Gwen. "When the baby is born, I'm going to divorce you," he declared. With those parting words he walked out of Cheryl's life.

The final month of Cheryl's pregnancy was like a black hole, a bottomless pit of devastation and depression into which she descended. Since her marriage she had isolated herself from all her own friends and had little contact with her family. She was terrified of the impending trauma of childbirth on her own and even more frightened by the prospect of going to court. She'd done all she knew to do in her relationship with Leo. She'd given up her friends, school, church, her own beliefs, and family contact to please him. Now he was abandoning her and their baby for an older woman and some other man's children.

Obviously, she reasoned, she just didn't know how to love. What was the use of living if no one loved her and she didn't have the ability to love anyone? She was tormented by the rejection and betrayal. The final month before her baby's birth was spent isolated in the house, physically surviving on a gallon of milk a day and two packages of cigarettes. Mentally she removed herself by allowing her childhood friend, "The Black," to come and swallow her up. No feelings, no pain.

A pinpoint of light came on August 30, 1978, just after her twenty-fourth birthday when her son, Ryan, arrived. It was Ryan that gave Cheryl the motivation to pick herself up again and continue her journey to wholeness. State law at that time did not allow Leo to file for divorce while Cheryl was pregnant. As soon as Ryan was born, he filed. Up until that point, Cheryl, reluctant to have another failed relationship in her life, had been willing to forgive and forget if Leo would return home.

When she realized he was going to remain with, and marry Gwen, she decided to fight back and not allow Leo to control her life anymore. She filed a countersuit on the grounds of adultery and the divorce was granted to her. The betrayal by Leo and the ensuing court battle during the divorce became the gel that congealed to strengthen Cheryl's backbone. This was going to be the last time she would allow herself to forfeit her own identity to please another person.

Still, she was desperately sad and very lonely. She'd thought Leo would be able to fill the emotional void of her childhood. Instead, he'd abandoned her and their baby. Ryan was her only reason for existence, and she knew that wouldn't always be enough. With no one else to turn to, she turned again to the only source of comfort she'd found as a child, her faith in God.

Sixteen
EPILOGUE –
WHATEVER HAPPENED TO ALL THE "KIDS"?

It seems that every time I speak or someone reads my mini-book or book, they always want to hear about how my siblings are doing. So here is a synopsis of each to let the reader know they are all "okay", but respecting their privacy.

DAVEY

Davey is still married to Sula, and they have settled in the northern United States. They lead a relatively quiet life, and both are still working at jobs they have held for many years. Their three children are grown and have re-established connection with them, and they are working on their relationships. It is a process but one that Davey desired and waited for patiently for many years.

EDDIE

Eddie never married, though he still holds out hope that someday he will find someone he loves and wants to marry. He also settled in the northern states and lives not far from Davey. Eddie has a successful remodeling business and has mentored many young men in the remodeling trades so they can establish their own businesses. He and Davey get together for cookouts and other outings. They often travel together for family gatherings with "the girls"– his sisters.

RICHIE

Richie stayed by the ocean after his retirement from the Navy and is currently in the home stretch of a second retirement from the shipyards. He considers his greatest life achievement to be his daughter, his only child. She has multiplied his joy with her three children, and Richie loves being a doting dad and grandpa.

KATI

Kati was able to have a miraculous eye surgery around her fortieth birthday. This opened a whole new world to her, and she pursued the education she had always wanted. She was the first of the seven siblings to get a bachelor's degree (graduating with honors), and will soon have a master's degree. She hopes to soon be certified to teach the blind. She and her husband have two grown sons and four grandchildren.

KARI

Kari survived numerous abusive relationships and eventually made peace with single life. She has a grown son. Kari and Kati live close to each other and only a couple hours away from Cheryl. A true survivor in every way, Kari also survived nine heart attacks and two angioplasty surgeries. After the initial heart attack that left Kari in a coma for ten days, the medical team encouraged Cheryl to take her off life support. Their diagnosis was that Kari would not be able to walk, talk or feed herself. With the whole back and tip of her heart irreparably damaged, her life expectancy was mere months. Amazingly, Kati sat up and came out of the coma on the tenth day. She was able to immediately come off life support instead of having to be weaned off. Years later she is finally pursing her dream of working in homeland security and will soon graduate with honors with a four-year degree in that field.

ROSIE

Rosie settled in the Midwest and has lived independently for many years. She has never married or had children, but has a host of four-legged felines that complete her family. She is active in her church and has a busy social life. She loves music and creative hobbies.

SEVENTEEN
CHERYL –
THE JOURNEY TO WHOLENESS FOR ME

The first part of this book I wanted to tell the story (from my point of view) of my childhood and some of the experiences that impacted my life, my thought processes, and who I became. When I left home at the age of seventeen, I was so angry and bitter. I wondered if I would spend my entire life being so mad!

It was a journey, a process, to get me past the abuse and into position to be able to forgive, to love and to be loved. I call it the journey to wholeness. There were so many people that contributed to that journey, but ultimately I helped myself the most. That might sound egotistical and prideful, but it isn't at all; it's just the way it was. It was the result of my choices, my discipline to take control of my thoughts, attitudes and actions. I'll try to explain.

There are four basic types of abuse: (1) Physical Abuse (2) Mental and Verbal Abuse (3) Sexual Abuse and (4) Neglect. All of these can produce emotional damage in the victim. It can be very difficult to gain and maintain a stable relationship with anyone when haunted by past negative circumstances.

There are certain areas in our soul (emotional) realm that need special healing that can only come at a deep spiritual soul level. Often there seem to be areas of our lives that fail to respond to self-discipline and sheer willpower alone, or even prayer. To reach a level of wholeness that lets a person recover from memories that cause pain and instability takes some re-learning, or re-programming – a change beginning at an intellectual level with thought processes.

There are so many clues that provide evidence of what I would call emotional damage. I find myself hesitant to even label it emotional "damage." The term seems to infer even more brokenness and irreparable impairment of an individual that likely already feels devalued. But for lack of a better description, it's what I use.

Things I experienced and have found many other survivors sense include a feeling of powerlessness, an inability to trust, a sense of unworthiness, super-sensitivity, and fearfulness. In an effort to counterbalance that, a lot of survivors have what I term "over-achiever syndrome." They (we) try to be the best at everything and wear ourselves out trying to please every person in our lives.

Many issues that can negatively impact our physical bodies and cause some mental distresses have a prescription available to ease the symptoms. The problem is that typically they do just that. They treat the symptoms without ever addressing the root cause. I had to get myself into position to confront and deal with why I thought, acted, reacted and viewed life and relationships in such an unhealthy way, even when I didn't know it was unhealthy. I just knew that I was a truly sad, angry, lost soul, and I did not want to live my entire life feeling that way.

Sometimes negative behaviors are not given up willingly, some are defended and actually come to be viewed as positive and justified. This includes anger, bitterness and unforgiveness. To me, these emotions seemed to bring about a sense of power and control over the things that had happened to me. They became a crutch, an excuse for present behaviors and circumstances.

It is difficult, if not impossible, to experience healing for damaged emotions until a person can accept responsibility for their own actions and behaviors in the present and stop blaming it on everyone in their past. Over time I began to see very clearly that healing comes after forgiveness.

There were a lot of other issues I had to get past before I felt I could get to forgiveness. One of the deepest desires of my heart was to be confident, sure, bold, hopeful, trusting and trusted. From my point of view, none of those virtues were within my grasp unless things changed.

We all have three basic needs: to love, to be loved and to be made to feel worthwhile. Because of my experiences growing up, I certainly didn't feel loved or worthwhile. I also believed that I didn't know how to love. If I was worthwhile, if I was lovable, why did all these bad things happen? Why had I been treated so badly? Was it a failure on my part in knowing how to love? My whole perspective on life and love was so distorted, so warped, that it seemed almost hopeless to ever be "normal."

It seemed that every time I made a conscious decision to change my actions, behaviors, and habits, things just got worse.

There were so many emotional debts (things that no one could make up for or fix in my past) that it seemed impossible. There had to be a way to take past wrongs and turn them around to use in a positive way in my life.

The measure of my worth had always been according to what had been done to me or said about me. It seemed that the way I viewed myself was reflected in how I conducted my life in relationships with others. You can guess how well that went. I was an emotional disaster waiting to ruin every significant relationship in my life. Something had to change or I was destined to spend my life in isolation and misery! My mindset had to change. I saw myself as pitiful and lost. Somehow I had to see myself as powerful and with a purpose. I saw myself as a victim, and every action and reaction was from a victim mentality. I needed to see myself as a victor and act like one.

Part of the process was allowing the light of truth to penetrate and reveal the darkness and to heal the hidden things that interfered with living a life of freedom and peace. Since I had no one person I could turn to that I felt could understand everything, I had to hold on to the hope that possibly God offered me unconditional love. I decided to believe that He wouldn't withhold His love until my behavior was acceptable. In a very small apartment, all alone in a new city, I made a kind of pact with a God that I had rejected, because He was all I had. Without this hope that maybe He did love me, I was utterly without hope.

You may not believe that is possible, but it's too late to tell me that! I believed, and step by step, piece by piece, the brokenness that was me--my life, my soul, my spirit--was slowly put back together.

There had to be healing in my mind because I had a distorted self-concept. There had to be healing in my thought processes because I was haunted by terrible images, guilt and bad memories. I had to learn to guard my thoughts as a lifestyle rather than it just being something I did when in crisis.

There had to be healing in my body. So many hurts were so seared into my mind, soul, and thoughts that they affected me physically. I saw a poster once that said "disease" in the body was directly linked to "dis-ease" in a person's soul. For me, it showed up in my physical appearance. I was anorexic before most knew what that was. It seemed I didn't deserve to even take good care of myself. That had to change.

There were so many emotions in me that I thought were sin. I was a very harsh judge of myself. I came to realize that no emotion is sin in itself, but the action/reaction I had to those emotions was important. Anger, rage, hatred—all of these are real emotions, sometimes buried by time, guilt, or humiliation. I found that emotions acknowledged, dealt with, and turned over to God could be constructive building blocks for emotional stability.

For me, true resolution only came through surrender of what my mind, intellect and emotions screamed I had a right to. I had to allow peace to come in and wash my soul and choose to lay all that emotional garbage down. Negative emotions are a heavy weight that will crush your soul and spirit and will be a barrier to wholeness. They simply are not worth holding onto.

For me, it was a system of choices that I had the power to make. Other survivors have those same choices. Did I want crippling fears or freedom? Would I choose cancerous bitterness that ate away at my own happiness, or would I let that go? Was it in my best interest to hang on to harmful resentments and ill will toward people in my past, or could I choose to never let that person(s) ever consume another minute of my life?

Here was a list of things I could choose to hang on to: damaged emotions, feelings of hurt and abandonment, a fractured mind-set, emotional conflicts, and difficulty in forming close relationships. How could I let go of all that and have a "normal" life? There were some people I had formed relationships with, but it seemed I always ruined them. I would look to that person (male or female) as my source for life, joy, and self-esteem.

It seemed that to be emotionally healthy no one person could be my source for those things. They became too overwhelmed and unable to fulfill all those needs and slowly weeded me out of their life, leaving me devastated and once again feeling unlovable.

There was a desperate need in my life, as it is to most people, to have solid, healthy relationships with God, immediate family members, extended family, work and social relationships. I had to choose to remove the things that poisoned my life so I could evolve from victim to victor.

***

Do you want to be set free? Do you want to be healed of the past? That seems like a ridiculous question, yet many times people are so used to operating in crisis mode they don't know how else to relate to people. Take away their infirmity and they are lost. Their identity is consumed with how damaged they are, how hurt they are, how needy they are. That was me.

How did I begin to be responsible for my actions? I found that I really could not receive healing for damaged emotions until I stopped blaming everyone else and accepted my responsibility to deal with my own issues, with the goal of moving forward. I had to make a conscious decision to move forward and not look back, except to learn from the past.

In time I found that I had to watch my motive in sharing past hurts with people. Was it because I want them to understand who I was and where I came from? Did I just want them to know what happened to me and feel sorry for me and then continue to relate to them in an unhealthy way? Sounds harsh, but sometimes it was true.

In studying the Bible and trying to learn more about God, I saw that guilt and condemnation are not the voice of God. It may be that my count is a little off, but resources I found listed the word condemnation in the Bible 12 times and righteousness 306 times. I chose to focus on righteousness.

Ask yourself, do you want to be pitiful or powerful? That was the question I used as a measure so many times. Do you want people to feel really sorry for you or rejoice with you at what you have been able to overcome? Do you want to be dysfunctional or set free from your past? Do you want to feel like your life is ruined forever, or do you want to rise up in righteousness, peace, and joy for what is left of your life here on earth?

I found that the measure of importance that I gave to truth in my life was the measure that it produced back in my life. For me, truth was found in what I studied in the Bible about how much God loved me and how He created me to be. Once I got a revelation of the power of my own words and my thoughts, it absolutely changed my life forever.

It is true that heredity, environment, and experiences all contribute to who we are, but they do not define who we can become. Though the abuses we have experienced may have been horrible atrocities, I say that everything I experienced helped make me who I am, and I like who I am. The past is not going to consume my future, because I choose for it not to. Anyone can make that same choice.

While it is true that a person can't just "get over it" (it is a process), there is a healthy way, a more productive way to work out things from your past. Simply re-hashing over and over again to temporarily sympathetic listeners only serves to keep that junk alive and still a destructive force in our lives. Right choices can make our mess our message, our stumbling blocks our stepping stones.

It seems true that you become like the people you spend time with. Have you ever noticed that couples that have married for many, many years seem to think alike, sound alike, and even talk alike? Years ago there was a commercial about dogs and people, and the advertiser showed people with dogs that looked like their owners. I determined that I wanted to be a reflection of my Heavenly Father. I wanted to fall in sync with His heartbeat and compassion for people. I tried to grasp hold of what I believed were His standards, His perspective, His heart, and His mercy and compassion. I prayed that every person within my sphere of influence could be blessed by my new higher perspective.

YOU ARE VALUABLE!

Many times we tend to let our worth be determined by the natural things, things that are temporal and subject to change--education, achievements, possessions, resources, or property. Other things that have been used to determine value are talents, skills, abilities, even physical appearance. This shallow value system has caused people to have a distorted view of what makes a person valuable. It leads to emotional pain and spiritually stunted growth because people don't know their own worth.

What are you worth? Please don't make the mistake of judging or valuing yourself according to the world's system or according to what you may see at the moment. I found that how I saw myself was extremely important.

A person's "self-talk" will be part of what forms their attitudes; their attitudes will come out in actions; actions will become habits; and habits help form destiny.

Our souls (emotions) are like fountains of life inside of us. They can be the filter and the force that pushes out all the garbage in our lives. The value of an item is sometimes concealed by garbage (dirt, dust, decay), but once it is cleaned up the true value can be revealed.

What kind of garbage is concealing your true value? Betrayal? Unforgiveness? Bitterness? Anger? Feelings of inadequacy? A sense of failure?

In years of dealing with people and trying to help them walk through devastating past experiences, it saddens me that people have difficulty loving and being loved. I understand, though, because I've been there. There have been so many painful experiences that often future expectancy is based on old, bad history.

While we can't change the past or make up for it, we can change our expectations, our attitudes, and our responses.

Coping with deep emotional wounds (from people that we trusted, loved, and people that should have loved us in return, nurtured us, protected us) can be very difficult.

There are so many hurting people who are emotional prisoners of their past. They become survivors when they finally realize that they hold the key to their own freedom. A survivor is one who is no longer a victim. The key is forgiveness, and the prison bars can only be unlocked from the inside.

Once a person has unlocked their heart, they can become free to love and be loved in a pure and right way. Victim/survivors many times, without realizing it, may require more of other relationships – trying to "make-up" for their losses. They require of their family, friends, and mates what these people cannot possibly do – fill the voids and emptiness inside. This wrong way of thinking places other people in a position of being like an idol. An idol is anyone you look to for life, joy, and self-esteem. Most people will be too overwhelmed and unable to fulfill all our needs. You can need another person in your life without being needy.

Even in the best of circumstances, parents can hurt their children. Brothers, sisters, other relatives, friends, co-workers, or friends may betray you. A spouse may reject you. When we have expectations that are too high for those around us, we can be sure they will not be able to always live up to what is expected of them.

Often we survivors ask from other people what they are incapable of giving. We try to make them fix for us what they cannot repair. We ask them to fill voids that they cannot fill.

Sometimes in our desperate need to be loved we only drive people away. Thank God we can get free from past experiences and from wrong or distorted thinking. Another person, no matter how special they are, is not capable of bearing the burden of fixing you or making you feel adequate, capable, able, loveable, and worthy. The burden is just too heavy. The weight of it will crush them and overpower every feeling they have for you. They will find you to be clingy, smothering, obsessed, suspicious, hostile, and jealous of others, too demanding – and you will again and again be rejected.

The healing process for me had to include the courage to root out the anger, bitterness, and rage, bring it out before God, and put it in the past, where it belonged. We can't control what happened to us in the past, but we do have power over our own thoughts, attitudes, choices, actions and reactions to circumstances.

Forgiveness will help you with your past, your present, and your future. It may seem to you a very difficult thing, but the fact is that your capacity to forgive will determine your destiny, your blessing, and your life benefits.

If a person holds onto unforgiveness, it results in bitterness and wrath. It is dangerous to your health to hold onto anger and unforgiveness. The high price of anger is dis-ease (disease).

Unforgiveness affects a person's body and health. Our bodies were not designed to withstand the pressures brought to bear by unforgiveness. We were created to operate in tranquility and peace. Unforgiveness is a poison to our systems. It produces the fruits of unforgiveness, and our bodies will respond appropriately. Headaches, neck pain, ulcers, fatigue, and depression can often be rooted in unresolved anger, bitterness, and unforgiveness.

The family of unforgiveness includes bitterness and wrath, strife, evil speaking, hatred, malice, jealousy, negative thinking, distrust, guilt, resentfulness, insecurity, being and staying grief stricken, anxiousness, and many other negative, unfruitful emotions that result in an inability to have confidence in ourselves or anybody else, including God.

If you've been abused, the greatest thing you can do for yourself is to forgive and let go. Healing is a process. Forgiveness is too. Forgiveness is not an emotion, it is a choice. Unforgiveness is a poison. It is like a cancer that consumes anything good and healthy in the host. My pastor once said, "Unforgiveness is like you drinking poison and expecting your enemy to die."

Harboring unforgiveness is the most destructive force a person can embrace. Most abuse survivors have always had a sense of powerlessness. They mistakenly believe that bitterness and unforgiveness are the only powers they wield over their abuser(s). The greatest sense of freedom and power I experienced was when I let go of the unforgiveness.

If you were training for the Olympics or just a local fun run, you would commit yourself to do whatever it took to accomplish your goal. Is your goal to be whole and healthy in your mind, soul, and emotions? Are you willing to commit to helping yourself?

Consider this: Has your soul, your emotional realm, been damaged by the abusive situations you've experienced? Were you injured? Hurt? Disabled in any area of your life? What would happen if your physical body had been damaged to the same degree? You would get some help! You would commit to a treatment plan – removal of the cause of the pain, surgery to repair the damage, a time of exercising good self-care, a regimen of medications, and perhaps some physical therapy. Exercise!

Commit to this critical part of the "treatment" – an offensive move that will put you through training that will change your lifestyle forever. It will equip you to make it through the future to walk in victory. You can come to believe and accept and walk in the truth that YOU can TAKE and KEEP control of your thoughts (especially those about yourself.)

The very qualities and personality quirks that helped us to survive can be tools that will make us strong in our own growth and in reaching out to help other hurting people.

Our thought life can turn our hearts in how we view our past life and how we view the person we are and can become.

Once we have begun walking in wholeness and victory, we can begin to reach out to others. Often the most effective reaching out we do first is to those we have hurt because we've been hurting. This is part of cleansing the damage of our past.

Whatever types of abuses have been experienced, the emotional damage may seem to linger long after the incidents and individuals who produced that damage are past. Emotional healing is a process.

I found the most healing experiences I had were in reaching out to others. It forced me to stretch and pull on my experiences with a different goal in mind. The focus turns outward instead of inward.

In reaching out to others, there comes a sense of strengthening in ourselves. We can begin to view ourselves from a different perspective. We can start looking back to help others begin to look forward. As we give of ourselves and share with others the things that have become revelation to us, they become even more real to us.

With a goal of helping others, our reference points broaden and we find we are no longer living in as narrow a world as we've previously been limited to. As we listen to others, we become less self-focused. In listening we also benefit because we receive affirmation that the responses we had to the things we experienced are "normal" – almost universal – considering all the abnormal and deviant things we may have gone through.

The foundation we've built in walking toward wholeness becomes a foundation upon which we can build unwavering stability. No longer do we have to waffle around trying to manipulate people or circumstances to accommodate all the losses we've experienced. We can impact those that come within our sphere of influence and help them begin to see that they too can walk in victory over abuse.

It is important to remember that in sharing experiences and listening to others, it's not a competition. I've been in situations sometimes where I hear someone share a painful experience and another person will say, "Oh that's nothing... you think that's bad, listen to this."

Always remember that no matter what someone has experienced – whether it's lesser or greater (from our perspective) than what we've experienced – to the degree it was painful and devastating to them, it was just as bad. Acknowledge their pain, let them feel safe in sharing with you and then direct them to what you've learned in the Bible that brought healing to your life. Share some experiences or things that others said or did for you that were healing for you.

The message that will speak the loudest will be living our lives in peace, happiness, joy and victory. The people usually that have watched our lives the closest are those who live with us—our spouses and our children. With other people we may tend to get a little "preachy" with our new-found freedoms, but that usually doesn't "fly" with those who live with us, those we may have hurt when we were still hurting.

Often we can't use words (apologies, regrets, etc.) to "fix" the times we've hurt those we love the most (those living with us). They may have heard those words from us before and they won't carry much weight with them. Be patient. Just living our lives before them with new coping skills, new perspectives of God, others, and ourselves will speak volumes to our families that will give new credibility to our lives.

They'll feel happier as they see us being truly happier. Most of the time our families have seen our pain, acknowledged it, tried to understand it, deal with it, help us with it – without success. They will be as overjoyed as we are – perhaps more so – with our journey to wholeness. Let them participate. It is comforting for them to be able to comfort someone they love deeply and to begin to see the healing, the changes, the growth and the freedom.

Part of the healing process is gaining a certain measure of understanding of how and why we react as we do in certain circumstances. Compassion is the companion of mercy, and with those come forgiveness, acceptance, and love. It's a chain reaction.

There is a cycle to abuse, but I like to believe that the cycle can be turned around and produce positive results. I have some friends – Don and Janet - that God gave a creative idea to. From that creative idea they designed a piece of equipment called a gasifier. It takes refuse (garbage) and through a process turns that garbage into energy that produces electricity. It also produces a rich potash that can be sold as a very beneficial fertilizer.

To me that is a picture of the healing process for us. God's love, mercy and grace mixes with our damaged emotions, our injured bodies, our broken spirits, and all the scars and crippling effects of abuse. (What a combination!)

Then, all that garbage in our lives that caused so much destruction and pain is turned into triumph and victory. We become instruments of praise and voices of victory – giving thanks for what we survived and how far we've come. We can then reach out a helping hand to other hurting people, because we know how wonderful it is to be set free of the past.

Some other friends of mine, Deborah and Joel also have a great example of redemption and exchange. They had a good business in the oil industry, but the thing that interested them most was buying and smoking marijuana. They enjoyed a life of partying and drinking and smoking pot on the weekends. During the week, they ran a respectable business.

One day they realized that their lives seemed empty and without purpose. They didn't want to give up the partying and drinking and smoking pot, but it just didn't seem to bring enough joy or happiness to them. One day they decided to visit the same church I attend. When they walked in, they immediately felt they were in a holy place. At the end of the service they went to the altar, and after prayer they felt such joy and expectation.

When they went home they knew they had to get rid of all the marijuana. That same night they lit a fire in their fireplace and threw it all in. It seemed like they sacrificed a lot when they gave up all that pot. It was worth a lot of money, and they depended on it to make their weekends fun! But they soon discovered that in its place they found a new love for God, for each other, and their fellow man.

From that point forward, their lives and their businesses were really blessed. After that weekend, they never again drilled a dry well. Their choice to lay down some things they thought were so important to them opened the door for them to receive back so much more than they gave up.

Soon, instead of consuming their resources on drugs and alcohol and partying, they were able to use their resources to have a blessed life, and to bless their families, their employees and many others. They went almost directly from pot parties to mission trips. For several years they were on most of the mission trips I was blessed to participate in all over the world. On those trips their love, their joy and their generosity blessed people all over the world.

To me this is a great picture of what I like to call a "divine exchange." They exchanged something in this world that they valued, and they got a divine exchange that was so much more profitable in their lives and the lives of everyone they meet. That's what we do when we "give up" unforgiveness. We lay that down, but the divine exchange means that we gain so much more that is so very valuable to us, our families, and every person within our sphere of influence!

We can't change or make up for the past, but we can have power and control over our futures and impact the futures of people within our sphere of influence. Isn't that amazing!? We are in control. We have the power of choice. We have the ability to change the course of our own lives, and through our lives we can help change the lives of many others.

"The joys of your future will swallow up the sorrows of the past."

Back when I first heard that sentence I never imagined I could ever be free. It never occurred to me that my life could matter, that I could do some things for God and others. Never before had I imagined myself in a position of helping other people. I had considered I could help each of my six younger brothers and sisters, which was a good start. With them I was motivated by mercy, compassion, understanding, acceptance, forgiveness, and love. All of those flowed because I knew my siblings, their lives, and their hearts, and I cared about them. I loved them.

As I opened myself to love for other abuse victims, there was that connection – deep to deep, spirit to spirit. It didn't matter if they were younger or older than me, richer or poorer, men or women, Americans or nationals from other countries. Because of that openness, I have had great mercy and grace and opportunities all over the world to share with people the freedom and joy that comes with forgiveness. You can make those same choices and have amazing opportunities of your own.

EIGHTEEN
THE WORLD CHAPTER OF MY LIFE

In nearly two decades of travel and ministry all over the world, I have seen so much. These experiences helped me gain a broader perspective of suffering and the power of the human spirit for survival. It also taught me great lessons on the power of forgiveness.

The pain and suffering humans inflict upon each other has been well documented. Visits to memorials dedicated to assuring those who suffered and are not forgotten have made my abusive childhood seem almost insignificant in comparison.

Their stories and faces became etched in my heart and in the memories of all who view these memorials. I have talked one on one, face to face, heart to heart with victims of all kinds of cruelties all over the world. It has greatly changed my perspective of what true abuse and suffering is. It has also been an inspirational journey to document the capacity each person has to forgive.

My forty-seventh birthday, June, 2001, Yad Vashem, Jerusalem. This is the Jewish people's memorial to the murdered six mil-

lion victims. Containing the world's largest repository of information on the Holocaust, Yad Vashem is a leader in Shoah education,
commemoration, research and documentation.

Upon entering the center, a somber reverence settles over the
shuffling groups silently passing through the rooms. Haunted faces, gaunt figures, fear-filled eyes stare back at visitors. Wide-eyed
little children with the golden Star of David on their sleeves hold
tightly to a helpless parent's hand. A pile of tiny shoes reminds us
that even the most innocent paid the ultimate price for crimes they
did not commit.

In Phnom Phen, Cambodia, a visit to "The Killing Fields"
memorial screams the details of crimes of man against fellow man.
The Killing Fields were a number of sites in Cambodia where
large numbers of people were killed and buried by the totalitarian
communist Khmer Rouge regime, during its rule of the country
from 1975 to 1979. At least 200,000 people were executed by the
Khmer Rouge. The best known monument in the Killing Fields
is Choeung Ek. Today, it is the site of a Buddhist memorial to the
terror.

In July, 2006, I stood in these places where the humidity and
heat were smothering. Standing in front of an old battle scarred
tree, a plaque says this tree is where children were beaten to death
to save bullets. I shudder with a sudden cold chill. Close by, at
Choeung Ek I raise my eyes toward the bright sun overhead. The
towering structure is filled with piles of skulls, bones, and tattered
pieces of clothing – a memorial to the thousands murdered by
blind hatred. Later that day I sadly walk through Tuol Sleng, a
high school that became a torture chamber for hundreds of fami-

lies. It is now a museum commemorating the genocide. I can see the horrible suffering in the stark black and white photos of victims' faces lining the walls.

August, 2007 – a hot summer day in Kigali, Rwanda – my translator points at a picture inside the Kigali Genocide Memorial. "That was my daddy. He was killed with a machete." I can hardly breathe. Taking her hand, we continue through the exhibits.

The Kigali Memorial Centre was opened on the 10th anniversary of the Rwandan Genocide, in April 2004. The Centre is built on a site where over 250,000 people are buried. These graves are a clear reminder of the cost of ignorance.

The Rwandan Genocide was the 1994 mass killing of more than 500,000 of Rwanda's Tutsis and Hutu political moderates by Hutus under the Hutu Power ideology. Over the course of approximately 100 days, from April 6 up until mid July, at least 500,000 people were killed. Most estimates indicate a death toll between 800,000 and 1,000,000.

The Centre is a permanent memorial to those who fell victim to the genocide and serves as a place for people to grieve those they lost. I walk through the memorial, looking at pictures and other items, overcome with emotion too powerful for words. Entering the room that is a memorial to child victims, I read about individual children. Each picture lists their name, age, and their favorite things. Looking at their beautiful baby faces I read how they died. Eyes gouged out, beaten to death, hacked to death... bodies six feet deep on the roads. I can no longer stay in the Children's Memorial Room. My guide, too, is overcome and has slipped outside.

Together we step across the back courtyard. From here we

see the hills of the city and a long black marble wall that lists the names of genocide victims. I put my arm around my guide and we walk away in silence, then we pray and cry together in the car.

My most significant memory of witnessing the pain and suffering of people came from a 1999 visit to Sierra Leone, West Africa. I visited and shot video in a refugee camp for amputees. It was a living genocide museum flaunting the horrible atrocities of their Civil War with the Rebels and the greed for the blood diamonds.

The first man I talked to was an amputee holding a fourteen-month-old baby girl. Her arm had been hacked off at the elbow by rebel forces. Another young man on crutches tells me to call him "Mr. T" because he is tough. It took six rebel soldiers to hold him down as they took an axe and cut off his left leg. A second young man, his two arms honed down to a point just past his elbows, tells me his story. It took three rebels to hold him down. They were going to chop off his right arm. He begged them, "Please, take my left arm. I am a student and the sole support of my family." Mercilessly they chopped off both arms. Gangrene set in before he got medical help and the dead flesh was scraped away leaving points with what was left of his arms.

Our team has brought in food, rice, prosthetics, literature and Gideon Bibles. There are over 600 victims living in this refugee camp. The camp leader is an amputee too. He stands up to speak and thank us for these benevolent gifts.

As he speaks, I shoot video footage. I feel intrusive watching men with missing arms and hands try to pull the sides of their shirts together as the wind blows through the tent. Young boys seated beside them have to help these grown men dress and go to the bathroom. I watch young mothers with stump arms try to place their babies in position to nurse. I'm usually not so emotional, but I cannot stop the flow of tears.

The camp leader says in broken English, "We are glady, but not too much glady for these gifts you bring to us. Most of all, we are glady for your love and for the message of the Gospel of Jesus Christ. We want to say 'thank you.' Thank you. We sing a song of praise for you."

The camera pans the faces and broken, torn bodies. The refugees stand up, supported by sticks, crutches and friends. They close their eyes and peace settles over their faces as they begin to sing, "Thank we now, we thank Thee, oh Papa God thank we. What You do for me, I will always thank Thee..."

The camera is zoomed in and I slowly pull out and watch as stump arms are raised to the sky, eyes closed, and faces are raised toward heaven. Caught away in the message of the song, these brave people are lifting their voices and slashed limbs in a symphony of praise. I can't bear to watch. As tears stream down my face, I can no longer intrude on their pure worship. I shut the camera off and turn away.

The camp leader came and placed his stump arm around my shaking shoulders. He took his good hand and wiped at my tears. "Don't cry for us." He is looking straight into my eyes, pleading. "If you cry, we have to cry. We've already cried our tears. The rebels... they are bone of our bone... flesh of our flesh. We forgive them. We have to forgive. If we don't..."

He lowers his head and as he turns me to face him, he takes me by the shoulders. "The rebels – we forgive them. We pray for them. They took our legs and our arms and our hands and our feet... but with forgiveness they can never have our soul or our spirit." In that moment I witnessed true forgiveness, and the strong spirit of man. It changed me forever.

I left home at age seventeen and walked my own journey toward wholeness through forgiveness. Learning that forgiveness is a choice, not an emotion, was a vital key. There have been many opportunities to choose to forgive. Because I did choose to forgive, I have been blessed to go to many, many countries, and most of them I visited several times over. I have shared with thousands and thousands of people my story and the message of the power of forgiveness. Had I not chosen to forgive, I would have sentenced myself to a slow and painful death for the rest of my life. Instead, I have been able to tell others about the power of forgiveness and to witness for myself other victims becoming victors.

Truly I believe that the power of forgiveness is embedded in every human spirit. We just have to let it rise up within us. Love, acceptance and forgiveness is the message of Jesus. The Bible says we're to be like Him. I've come to believe that the revelation of that is what brings healing to our own spirits, our soul and emotions. Our capacity to love is in direct proportion to the revelation of what forgiveness is in our lives.

It seems to me that our spirits were divinely designed to love, to accept and to forgive. When we justify other things like unforgiveness, bitterness, anger and wrath, we cannot find peace, and our capacity to love and to be loved is crippled.

When I recognized the gift of mercy, grace and forgiveness that was provided for me with Jesus' sacrifice, there was no other option but to choose to forgive. I choose to forgive. I choose to love. I choose to live. Those choices I believe have inspired others to forgive, to love, and to live. Those choices let me get better instead of staying bitter.

It has been a blessing to me to be inspired by the stories of people all over the world that have suffered yet triumphed because of their choices. Their sorrows diminish with time and healing, and those who choose to forgive don't have the barricade of unforgiveness blocking them from experiencing future joys.

The joys of my future did swallow up the sorrows of the past. There are still more joys ahead for me, and as you choose to forgive, you will also have more joy!

Nineteen
The Colors in my Life Rainbow

In trying to determine how best to end the book, there just wasn't a way I could make peace with. Then one morning I awakened with this whole "Rainbow" chapter in my head. Rainbows have always been very important in my life. It seemed they always came when I needed encouragement most. Color also was very symbolic for me. So in summing up the victorious chapter of my life, I have chosen to share stories of people I met when telling my story around the world. These incredible stories are from people that impacted my life, because they allowed me to impact theirs.

RED – BAMBI – SIERRA LEONE

Bambi was a young man I met in Makeni, Sierra Leone, West Africa. It was 1998 and the rebels had descended on his village and massacred his entire family in front of him. It was hard to imagine this handsome, smiling young man in front of me had witnessed and experienced such horror. But his body bore witness to the crimes of abuse. His arms had been cruelly amputated with a machete, cut off halfway between the wrist and elbow. He had heard my story in the big outdoor crusade, and the Bible school leader brought him to me for an interview.

Bambi said he had heard my story on forgiveness and wanted to tell me his story. It had been a year since his family had been murdered in front of him. He was only eighteen at the time.

With machetes the rebels slaughtered his entire family in a killing frenzy that lasted only a few minutes. They chopped off both of Bambi's arms midway between the wrist and elbow. Then the rebels somehow got distracted and ran outside. Bambi used the opportunity to escape. Desperately he ran with all his might, away from the screams and terror, leaving a trail of blood. The sun was sinking on the horizon and he had been running for a while. Bambi was weakening, and his heart pounding in terror kept the blood pouring down what was left of his arms.

He fell to his knees on the side of the road, still trying to hold up what was left of his arms. Suddenly a man appeared and stood in front of him. Bambi knew about God, but this man said his name was Jesus, and he was there to help Bambi. He told him how to tear his shirt with his teeth and tourniquet his arms, and assured Bambi he would guide him to safety.

Bambi felt new strength surge through his body and felt somehow comforted by this stranger's presence. Suddenly the man was gone, but Bambi now knew what direction to go. He made it to a refugee center and got medical help. The Germans sent a medical team to Bambi's refugee camp. They did surgeries on the refuges that helped them regain small use of their hacked off limbs. Bambi's surgery had separated the muscle of his forearms so that he could pick up objects and feed and dress himself.

Some months later he met a missionary and learned about the man he had met on the road – Jesus – someone he had never heard of, and then he truly realized what a miracle he had experienced.

As Bambi told me his story, his whole face was just glowing with joy and peace, especially as he related the part about Jesus, the man he had never known or heard of, that rescued him on that road. He was attending Bible school, and the school director said Bambi was their most excited, exuberant student. He was a strong leader and a messenger of hope to all who knew him.

So Bambi is RED to me – a reminder of the blood that he shed, but the life and joy he brought to others' hearts as he shared his heart and the power of the help that Jesus gave him. People may doubt Bambi's story and his experience, but Bambi doesn't mind. It's real to him, and that encounter on the road running away from Makeni changed him forever. Now Bambi's life and story are changing others' lives.

ORANGE – ASTRYD - HAITI

Astryd was standing at the front of a massive crowd in Haiti, listening to the music and preaching in an outdoor crusade. The people were standing shoulder to shoulder and constantly shifting, trying to get closer. As I told my story from the tall platform, I made eye contact with her several times. Amazing, considering there were likely over 50,000 people in the open soccer field, and I really tried to see and connect with all of them. She looked to be about eleven or twelve, in a simple threadbare orange dress and dusty, broken shoes. She had a lot of small, colorful ties in her hair and held a rag doll close to her heart.

I finished my part of the service and the preacher took the microphone and called for the people to begin to pray. Suddenly we heard a lot of noise just below the platform. I stepped forward and looked over the edge. A mass of people had formed a circle around someone who was screaming. They were screaming back and yelling and waving wildly. I couldn't understand a word. Our pastor stepped over to the disturbance and asked the crowd to stand back from the screaming person.

There, writhing on the ground, arching her back, jerking her head, flailing her arms and legs, and frothing at the mouth was Astryd. People screamed in English, "She has demons!" "Her grandfather is a witch doctor." "She has brought voodoo curses to this place. Cast her out!" Dozens of people started screaming at her again and saying loud, mean-sounding words in Creole, pointing at her and making angry faces. She jerked even more violently and screamed so wildly; it raised the hairs on my arms.

Pastor Billy Joe turned to me and said, "Cheryl, go down there and get her. Take her back by our ministry van and hold her and pray over her. Keep everybody else away from her. She is afraid. She needs to feel like she is in a safe and peaceful place."

Security helped me get to her and they carried her back behind the platform to the ministry van. It was no easy task! She kept writhing and screaming and kicking. It was very hot and humid. We both were sweating profusely. I held her in my lap and just kept praying softly over her and singing soothing songs as she screamed and jerked.

After what seemed a very long time, the Pastor came with a

translator and security, who had found Astryd's family. Through them we learned that Astryd had been cruelly abused in every way by her immediate family. Her grandfather was a well-known voodoo witch doctor, and she had been used in rituals from the time she was a tiny little girl.

City officials had finally somehow removed her from the village and her immediate family, and an aunt and uncle had custody of her. She had just turned twelve. They said she acted out like this frequently and that she had attacks like this many nights.

We prayed for her and talked with her through the translator. She began to calm down and finally quit screaming. The Pastor said, "Astryd, I know terrible things have been done to you, and for that I am truly sorry. Now you have a home where you are safe, and you are free from that abuse. I need to ask you to do something that may seem very, very difficult, but it will help you for the rest of your life. God will deal with the people who did these things to you. Your part is to forgive. It will bring peace to you. Just say these two words, 'I forgive.' It takes just two little words, spoken from your heart."

Astryd looked up at me. I was still holding her on my lap. She pressed hard against me. Finally she was not fighting me. I nodded my head and said, "You can do it, you can say those words." She sat up and tried to speak. She was so hot and sweating, but her mouth was crusted and dried up. I gave her my bottle of water and she drank the whole thing. Then, looking directly into Pastor Billy Joe's eyes, she said in a whisper, "I forgive."

Her whole body went limp and she closed her eyes. Everyone was suddenly very still and totally silent. I picked up a wet rag and carefully, softly wiped her face. As she slowly opened her eyes, a big smile broke across her face. It was like she lit up from the inside. She hugged me and then jumped up and ran to embrace her aunt and uncle.

For the next hour I got to talk with her and listen to her story. I encouraged her that I would be an ocean away, but God was as close as her heartbeat. She would never be truly alone. I never saw her again, but I like to believe that she got to live a life of peace from that night forward. Orange reminds me of Astryd, because of her orange dress, but also orange is like fire – and the fire of the hell she had experienced in that voodoo village was put out that night by the rain of peace, love and forgiveness.

YELLOW – VALENCIA - RWANDA

We had been in Rwanda for three days. We had taken in humanitarian aid and held nightly crusades in an open field. The field dipped down like a large bowl. Several hundred people stood down in the field, but many hundreds more lined the top of the rim, watching, listening every night.

The team had been through the Kigali Genocide Memorial and learned firsthand the horrible atrocities of that horrific 100 days in 1994 when over a half million Rwandan people were murdered. We didn't know it until Valencia came to the platform, but the very field where we were standing had been a makeshift refugee camp when military help finally arrived.

Valencia heard my story of the power of forgiveness and how the act of forgiveness (by faith, not emotion) can set a person free. She came to the platform to tell her story. She was eight years old when her mother, father and siblings were slaughtered. She witnessed it, hidden in the darkness, but managed to escape to her aunt's house. From that time on her aunt had raised her as her own child. That was in 1994.

Now, in 2007, Valencia stood on the stage and, with tears streaming down her face, said, "I have been so very angry. I have lived all these years with such anger and hatred in my heart for those who killed my family. I thought that I will never again capture the happiness and peace that I had before those men took away my family."

"But tonight, I heard the story of Cheryl, and I have hope that my life can now change for the better. So when the Pastor said to pray the prayer of forgiveness, I did this. I want to stand here before you and say that for the first time since my family was murdered, I am feeling peace. There is a burden lifted from my heart. This burden has been a weight on my spirit so that I can never feel happy or feel joy. Somehow tonight, though, I am feeling peace and happiness."

"Now I stand before you to say to my friends who have also felt such bitterness and anger as I have felt, you must forgive. We must forgive and go on. Our families are not coming back to us, but we are alive. We are alive and we must begin again to act as though we are alive. Before I came here tonight, I was dead. Now, thanks to God, I am alive."

I will always remember the joy that was so obvious on Valencia's face, even as the tears streamed down. Pastor Billy Joe and his wife, Sharon, prayed with Valencia, hugged her and encouraged her. I think the amazing thing is that Valencia saw beyond herself and immediately wanted her fellow Rwandans to experience the freedom that she found that night.

It is hard to imagine the pain and sorrow she must have experienced as a tiny little eight-year-old girl, suddenly robbed of nearly every person she loved so much. Years went by and she was still suffering and carrying such a heavy load for such a young woman. Yet, as an act of faith, she chose to say, "I forgive." It brought light and life, peace and joy to her immediately. It so flooded her soul and spirit that she was driven to get to the platform and compel others like her to forgive and experience what she did.

Valencia is the "yellow," the light and sunshine in my world experiences rainbow. I believe she is still shining that light into some very dark places and bringing freedom to everyone as she shares her story.

GREEN – ANNA – KAZAKHSTAN

As we went through customs in Kazakhstan, there was a commotion in the line next to us. Our pastors were being escorted out by security! A little while later we learned that they had brought the wrong passports with them and did not have a Visa. Therefore, they were denied access to the country. They had to fly back to Germany where someone from America brought the proper passports with Visas so they could come back to Kazakhstan in a day or two.

As television producer/videographer for the ministry, I knew the schedule called for them to speak in a very large church that evening. The people in Kazakhstan were very excited to hear them. The "Victory In Jesus" program with them had been airing for the past month, and the meeting was well advertised. I said, "Who is going to speak?" The answer, "You!"

Oh my goodness! They were expecting the Daugherty's – famous American television ministers, and they were going to get me, the TV person. Yikes! I was used to speaking, but I knew that I would be a huge letdown for the people who were expecting them to come to the meetings.

That night I was introduced and came to the platform following an introduction that I did not understand in their language. The translator was very positive, telling me that the people were excited to hear me. Sure, I thought. The audience did seem to be very responsive and listened intently as I told my story. At the end, the altar was crowded with people who wanted prayer. It had gone better than I could have hoped or prayed for!

After the meeting, the translator told me that the audience was delighted that I was the replacement for the pastors. Unknown to me, a program called "The Power of Forgiveness" had just aired that week in Kazakhstan. It was a dramatized video of my story and testimony and an interview with me. So, before I even came, they already felt that they knew me!

The next day, thankfully, our pastors were back, and I could focus on my job as the television person. After a luncheon, the host pastor approached us and asked if I could be excused to come and spend an hour or two with a young twelve-year-old girl they wanted me to visit with on an urgent matter.

The young girl's name was Anna. Her stepfather was a pastor and she had just the month before finally reported that he had been sexually abusing her for the past five years. The reason she finally came forward was she had witnessed him abusing her younger sister and also another little girl in the church. She wanted to protect them from the horrible things she had experienced for so long.

That revelation caused a big upheaval in their church and family. The stepfather was in jail, and a trial was coming soon. Anna felt that everything was her fault. She felt it was her fault that the family had fallen apart and her mother had lost a husband, and her siblings had lost their father. Other victims in the church had come forward, and the church disbanded and joined with the host church where we had been invited.

Anna had watched my story on television the week before. She prayed that very night and said, "God, if You are listening and really care about me, you can make a miracle for me, so that I can somehow speak with this lady, Cheryl."

One week later, she came to church with her mother, and when the special speaker was announced, I stepped up onto the platform. Anna was so overwhelmed. She knew that it was a specific answer to her prayer, the miracle she had asked God for. Her mother was friends with the host pastor, and they arranged for a meeting with me.

I spent over two hours with Anna, along with her mother and a translator. She asked me all the questions that were so heavy on her little heart. She asked such deep, penetrating, hard questions that forced me to go to places I had not been myself for years. I answered all her questions and together we cried and talked about all the forbidden things that torment in those types of situations.

Afterward, we hugged and took pictures. I wanted to give her something personal and didn't have much with me. I took off my earrings and put them on her. Then, my friends Deborah and Joel and I collected our money and presented it to Anna's mother. It turned out to be exactly the amount of money they needed to go to a shelter and place of healing in another city. There was enough to pay for the journey and pay their expenses for the entire family for the ninety days they would be there. Anna and her mother were absolutely overjoyed at their miracles.

When I relayed her story to our pastors, Pastor Billy Joe said, "You know, if we came to Kazakhstan, and then had to return to Germany and come back again, only for Anna to get her miracle answer to prayer, it was worth it."

Our trip to Kazakhstan brought hope and life to Anna and her family. So to me, Anna is green – symbolic of life… a new life, free from abuse. Thank God!

BLUE – NATALIA – RUSSIA

Natalia was a Russian orphan that I actually first met in Ka zakhstan. She was working as photographer for the host pastor there. She had been abandoned in Russia by a drug-addicted mother at age four. She was in many different, very bad situations and had been terribly abused. After she turned twenty-one, she got a work opportunity with her photography and had been living for a couple of years in Kazakhstan.

Because I was the videographer and photographer for our ministry team, she felt an immediate connection with me. After she heard my testimony and some of my experiences, she became my little shadow. The host pastors and others remarked that she looked like a young version of me. I had to admit that even I saw the resemblance!

She spoke Russian and Korean, and I spoke only English and a few Russian phrases, but we did manage to communicate with pictures and gestures and sometimes a translator. Over the course of the few days there we did form a bond and kept in contact.

After a few months, Natalia decided that like me, she had to take action and reach out to help other survivors. Those dearest to her heart were the many Russian orphans. She decided to give up her position of comfort and return to Russia. A series of divine connections put her in contact with an American missionary couple who needed an assistant, and Natalia returned to Russia.

Now she is established back in St. Petersburg where she herself once roamed the streets as an abandoned child. She has gained legal custody of three young teenage girls and has others that spend the weekends with her. She works with an orphanage and the children's ministry at a church.

We have remained in contact and I get to mentor and encourage her from a distance. Natalia is blue to me – true blue. Blue to me represents faithfulness, and she has been faithful to try to "pay it forward" for the blessings she has received.

All through her life growing up there seemed to be so little she received; no parents, love, safety, permanent home, or even necessary material things. Instead she was beaten, used as a servant, abused, and sexually molested in the homes that were supposed to provide her safety.

Natalia could be bitter and angry and trying to fill the empty places with drugs and alcohol and meaningless relationships. Instead, she has chosen a life of giving and pouring into other young girls what she herself never had. Because of those choices, her life is blessed and happy, and she is a vital part of giving so many other orphaned Russian girls love and hope.

INDIGO– CELESTIA – DOMINICAN REPUBLIC

It had been a very long week of outreaches and crusades and meetings in the Dominican Republic. It was one of the few that we did not have a medical team with us. We wanted to come back and bring more resources and medical and dental clinics. I decided to go to some of the Haitian refugee camps in the area to get some footage to create a video that could help raise funds to bring in more resources.

My driver and translator took me to three camps, and I took pictures and video and gave away little toy cars, super balls, Frisbees and gum and candy to the children. The driver said he knew of one more camp, but I decided we had enough footage. A couple miles down the road I said, "Turn back, I think we should go."

This camp looked the same as the others. I took a few pictures, but I was now out of toys and candy, so we left. As we were pulling away I noticed a tiny little girl standing by the gate. I stopped the driver and we got out to take a picture. She was Haitian, about three years old, but she was mulatto with a little blonde in her hair (caused by malnutrition) and crystal clear deep blue eyes.

I dug deep in my camera bag and found some candy and a balloon. A lady came running up to me, pulling on me and pointing to the tiny girl. She lifted up the little girl's dress and was pointing and talking rapidly with my translator.

The little girl's name was Celestia. She was three years old. The little girl with the lady was Angelica. She was Celestia's six-year-old sister. The mother was eighteen and had disappeared from the refugee camp three days earlier. The lady said Celestia refused to leave the gate, waiting for her mother to return. Of course they had no provisions. The lady said she had been giving them water and about a cup of rice a day. It was all she could spare. She had to feed her own children.

She lifted the little tattered dress and revealed a gaping hole in Celestia's side. Before she left Haiti, Celestia had had a colostomy in a clinic. In the journey across the mountains to the refugee camp, the tubing had fallen out. Body waste and infection was oozing out of the hole and down Celestia's side. Her little belly was swollen and bloated and her eyes looked jaundiced and glazed with fever or malaria.

I sent the driver to get some food and water and gave some money to the lady and told her we would send back help. I talked with Angelica and complimented her as the older sister taking care of little Celestia. I promised we would be back with help, and we would try to find their mother. As we pulled away, I could see the doubt in Angelica's eyes, but Celestia believed.

Alan, an American missionary working in the Dominican, promised he would go back and try to find Celestia and Angelica and get her to a doctor, but he said it would be a miracle to find her with so many hundreds of children. The thing that would help the most was her deep blue eyes, her lighter skin, and the lightness of her hair.

Thankfully, he did find Celestia and Angelica and a week later their mother returned. Alan was able to find a woman doctor willing to treat Celestia, but of course it would take money. The doctor said that without treatment, Celestia had only a few weeks to live. We knew we had to do something quickly.

With the help of my friends Deborah and Joel, and other U.S. partners in my ministry and with Alan's hard work on the Dominican side, we were able to send enough money to provide food and fresh water and medications for Celestia and her mother and siblings.

In just a couple of weeks she had improved enough for the surgery. Again we sent money for the entire family to travel with Alan to another city for the surgery. Miraculously the doctor was able to repair things so that Celestia no longer required the colostomy bag.

The doctor fell in love with Celestia and Angelica and they began to spend weekends with the doctor and her family. Soon the doctor was able to provide for them to have a place of their own and for the girls to go to school.

Two years later I returned and they arranged a meeting for me with the little girls and the doctor who treated Celestia. Now she is a happy, active little girl who loves school and loves God, and loves the doctor who saved her life.

Celestia is indigo to me because her deep blue eyes made it possible to find her – a little needle in a refugee haystack that might have died unnecessarily if I hadn't listened and gone back to that camp.

PURPLE – RYAN – USA

My "signature" and favorite color is purple, so of course my son and only child Ryan has to be the purple in my rainbow. When I got pregnant with him it was kind of a miracle considering all the abuse my body had experienced. Then to go through a difficult pregnancy and a marriage that ended in adultery one month before his birth could have made for a poor start in our relationship.

On that Labor Day weekend that he was born, so was a new start for my life. I held that tiny little man in my arms and knew that together we could make it. He was my motive for life, and my drive to be a stronger, better person.

There had been so much failure in my life that I determined that Ryan would be a success for me. I read all kinds of books on raising children, went to seminars, and allowed myself to be mentored in parenting. Those who had the most input into my life during that time were my pastor's wife, Sharon, my spiritual mother Patty, and various friends that all had experienced wonderful childhoods.

I was twenty-four years old with no husband or family support around, so everywhere I went, Ryan was with me. I bought a book called Let's Make a Memory written by several well-known ministers' wives. It gave so many wonderful creative ideas on how to celebrate holidays, special events and just everyday life. Though we were relatively poor, somehow I managed to do extra jobs and stash away money so that every summer we took some kind of vacation trip. Since I had very few pictures of my childhood, I made sure Ryan's was well documented!

Most importantly, though, I wanted to be sure that Ryan knew he was safe and loved, and that his needs, his dreams, his desires were heard and supported. I wasn't always the perfect mother, (and I tried to be a good "dad" too) but it wasn't for lack of effort.

Every decision I made as to where we lived, where I worked, socializing, and dating all revolved around what was best for Ryan. For a short time after the divorce, I dated but then I stopped. I saw that I was investing time in men that would later mean nothing to me. In return I was losing time with my child that I could never get back. It just wasn't worth the sacrifice.

Ryan was a wonderful child that was so happy and full of joy. As he got older he would sometimes get in trouble at school, not because he was disrespectful, but because he found school boring. He thought it was his personal responsibility to make sure everyone had fun at school, and he was very creative in how he made that happen. It often didn't set well with the teachers, but they did have to admire his efforts.

He was very artistic and creative from the time he could pick up a color or an instrument. It helped because I also always wanted to make things. We were a great team, and I made it my goal for us to learn a new skill every year.

So many times I could have made self-destructive decisions or tried to run away from problems and challenges, things I was afraid of. The only thing that drove me and kept me going was my love for that little boy. I knew that I was the one who loved him the most and that no one else could take my place. That in itself was kind of a miracle because in every other area I still had very little self-esteem.

I remember taking Ryan to a big Easter drama when he was three years old. I was holding him on my lap, and he loved all the singing and celebration as Jesus came riding in on a donkey. Later he got very upset during the beating of Jesus and the soldiers putting him up on the cross. I whispered to him, "Don't worry, it's not the real Jesus – he is just playing. Soon he will come out of the tomb." He seemed a little comforted, but he kept being worried. I noticed that he kept putting his hand up under his shirt and vest. I thought maybe his little bow tie was bothering him.

Soon, just as I had promised, Jesus came walking triumphantly out of the tomb and Ryan clapped and rejoiced with the rest of the audience. As we were driving home, he said, "Momma, I know that wasn't the real Jesus." I asked him why, and his answer brought tears to my eyes. He said, "Well, I know it wasn't the real Jesus because I kept touching my heart, and I never felt Him leave my heart."

As with most parents, I thought it was my job to teach him everything I knew and everything that could be important in his life. It seemed an overwhelming task, but that moment encouraged me so much. In reality it was Ryan that taught me so much as he was growing up.

There was a short period of rebellion when he was a teenager, but the counselor told me that was actually healthy, since we had such a close relationship. I'm not sure I believe that, but I am thankful that because of—and in spite of–me, Ryan grew up to be a fine young man that I am very proud of. He is absolutely the smartest, most talented, loving son a mother could ask for. Of course, that is said without bias!

He's made me cry a few times – and that's not all bad! I cried when he surprised me at a band concert with a solo on the alto sax. He was in the sixth grade and kept his solo a secret until the concert. The same thing happened when I watched him perform in the starring role of a passion play for missions. When he began his career as a videographer, I was overwhelmed with his talents, creativity and inspiring projects.

There were so many moments that are precious memories to me, and it is such a blessing that I can look back on his childhood with few regrets. There is a cycle to abuse, and my greatest goal was to make sure I never abused my own child. I was determined to break that cycle. I know for us that cycle is broken. Someday when the time comes I am also confident that Ryan will be a wonderful father to his children. He has already said that he knows what it was like to grow up without a father and he has a goal like mine, to be the best dad a child could ever have. To me, that is success.

I thank God that he blessed me with a son, and trusted me with that precious life. Ryan was the best gift God gave to me as a young woman. I'm not sure that I could have survived or been motivated to complete the journey to wholeness without him. When I finally met my soon-to-be-husband, Tom, it was Ryan who gave me a big thumbs up. He said, "Mom, I think this guy is smart enough to take you on, and I can tell he loves you too." Ryan represents purple to me – an inheritance, royalty (Ryan's name means laughing and happy little king) and the blessings of God.

GOLD – TOM
MY REWARD AT THE END OF THE RAINBOW

My husband Tom is truly the greatest gift God ever gave to me. I had to wait until I was fifty years old to meet and marry him. For twenty-six years I was a single-parent mom. For a long time I prayed for the right man to come along and sweep me off my feet and make my life complete. After a few years, though, I found that I wanted to have a life that was happy, satisfying and complete without a partner. It was important to me that once I did marry someone, if I ever did, that I would come into their life at a time when I didn't need to be rescued.

God blessed my life because of the choices I made, and when I met Tom my life was happy, satisfying. I could have been content to live out the rest of my life exactly as it was at that time. I was television producer for a large ministry that did a lot of outreach. I was blessed to get to travel to over thirty countries, many of them multiple times as the videographer for humanitarian outreaches and crusades all over the world.

But, a month before my fiftieth birthday, I made a trip to Hawaii with Patty, my spiritual mother, and Doris, a mutual friend. It was my fiftieth birthday year, Patty's seventy-fifth, and Doris' sixtieth. What a trio. I had just completed a forty-day juice fast and took the trip. Early mornings I would walk the beach and pray. In that prayer time I talked to God and said, "This is my 50th year – my jubilee year. If You have a husband out there who can love me and take me as I am, You need to send him to me this year. If not, then I am going to presume that You want me on the mission field, and I will retire to Sierra Leone (the country that touched me most) and live the rest of my life there."

I made peace with that decision and returned home. For my actual 50th birthday celebration in June, my son Ryan planned a big party. He invited friends and family from all over. He asked them to bring a card or a letter that told a funny or touching memory about their relationship with me so that I could have a collection of memories from all of them. Ninety-four people came to that celebration, and it was a wonderful time. I also received gifts on a money tree that allowed me to buy a special digital camera that I wanted. I knew it would help capture faces I loved from all over the world.

One of Ryan's gifts to me was a trial membership to an online Christian dating site. I was not too excited. But I did try it. The first person that popped up was Tom! I communicated with him and a few others, but no one else interested me. After about a month of communicating on e-mail, we finally met at church and had our first date. We went to eat at a Mexican restaurant, and our conversation lasted over four hours. It seemed like only a few minutes. We had to leave a really good tip for the waiter!

Tom was a widower and had been a pastor for many years. He had three daughters from his marriage. His wife's name was also Cheryl and her middle name was Lynn – both the same as mine. She had been diabetic and over time developed other diseases and complications from the diabetes. During that time, though, she did all she could to support Tom in ministry and was a wonderful loving mother to their girls.

They had several foster children they cared for over the years.

They also had a needy teenage girl that came to their church. Her parents were deeply involved in drugs. She was desperate to get out of that environment. Though Tom was only 29 years old, and Cheryl was only 27, they took her into their home. Tom knew they would get no financial help to keep her in their home, but they could not turn the 15 year old away. To me this shows the heart of Tom. During a time that he was so young and already had much responsibility, he was still willing to take on more because he cared about this girl that had been living in a bad environment.

When Tom's first wife Cheryl got too sick to work, he was her primary caregiver until she passed away. Tom says, "Unless you've done it, you cannot understand what it is like." To me it was the ultimate gift of unconditional love in a marriage. The morning before she stepped over into eternity, she thanked Tom for his love and care. They both had remained true to their vows of "until death do us part." They had been preparing to say "good-bye" for a very long time, but it was still a difficult time. Although he was so very sad to lose her, he was truly relieved that she no longer was suffering.

Months later when we met, Tom had to get past the part that I was divorced because he did not believe in divorce. Though I was divorced by circumstance (adultery), not by choice, it still was a hurdle for him. It helped him to know me, and he really respected that I had made a decision that raising my child was more of a priority than dating. He also really respected the fact that I had made a commitment to celibacy and purity during those twenty-six years of being single again.

After that four-hour lunch where we first met face to face, we were together every opportunity possible. He lived over a hundred miles away, and we alternated weekends between Oklahoma and Arkansas. My friends made accommodations for him when he was in Oklahoma, and his mom even re-did her spare room so I had a special place to stay. Within a short time we were engaged and got married seven months after our first date.

Tom is the perfect match for me, and he says I've been perfect for him. He is the sweetest, most loving man I have ever known. Before we were married, I would talk to my friends about him and almost every sentence started with, "He is so WONDERFUL." Now several years later, I feel the same, just to a greater degree.

Living with Tom these past few years has only been a daily confirmation of how blessed I am that I waited for someone like him. He is everything and more than I ever dreamed of, hoped for, prayed for, believed for and ... well, you get the picture!

He is my husband, partner, confidant, lover and closest friend. The sound of his voice brings me peace, and his touch is so comforting and reassuring. I respect him and have confidence in his integrity, and I trust him and his leadership. After waiting so very long for the "right" man, I cannot imagine my life without him. I still thank God every night that He let me be married to such a perfect husband for me. Tom truly has been my reward for the choices and sacrifices I made during the twenty-six years I waited for him to find me. He feels the same way about me.

Through his daughters we have been blessed with grandchildren and that has increased our joy. We have so enjoyed loving them, watching them grow and being a part of their lives. Only God knows how much more our joy will be expanded in the future!

A friend asked me not long after we were married, "What is the best thing about being married?" The answer came quickly and easily for me, and it's so true. I said, "The best thing about being married is that I know how wonderful the rest of my life will be." If I were going to write a song about our marriage I would title it "I've Been More Than Loved." With Tom I feel loved, valued, adored, wanted, protected, safe, equal, accepted and complete. It is truly such a wonderful life.

In this book you have read my story of "Seven Silent Witnesses" and heard the stories of the seven colors of the rainbow in my life. It seems amazing to me that because I chose to break the silence, I got to be a vital part in so many others breaking their silence and taking the steps to walk in the power of forgiveness. Any one of the seven of us could have been the first, but somehow I was the one. I find it incredible that my life was so very blessed after all. From the depths of despair and physical and emotional poverty, my life has become so rich in every way. In the beginning my siblings and I were held together by a powerful bond of silence, now we can all (including you, dear reader) be loud witnesses to the power of forgiveness.

Thank you for reading

Seven Silent Witnesses

You can visit our ***SEVEN SILENT WITNESSES***
Facebook page and "LIKE" us.

Please leave your comments for the author and other readers.

Write an e-mail to Cheryl at ***sevensilentwitnesses@yahoo.com***
We want to hear your thoughts and stories.

Most everyone knows someone who has been directly
or indirectly affected by abuse of some kind.
You may want to recommend this book to them,
or purchase extra copies to give away.

*For information about having the author speak to your
organization, group or church, please e-mail us.*